Fraud and White-Collar Crime

Fraud and White-Collar Crime

Frederick Oughton
Fellow of the Royal Society of Arts

Elek

Published in Great Britain by
ELEK BOOKS LIMITED
2 All Saints Street
London N 1

ISBN 0 236 15409 5

By the same author:

MURDER INVESTIGATION
Elek Books, 1971

Printed in Great Britain by A. Wheaton & Co., Exeter

Contents

This book is for

Rhian and Ruth

and for

my mother and Christine

A word to the people in this book

Friends,

When this book was first hatched up in the form of a mere idea, Tim Chilvers, the editor, was silent for a long time, and he then suggested that I write a specimen section. This I did, and it turned out to be Chapter Five, about how to fiddle a bank loan, and it was duly inspected by a banker, who said that this type of fiddle had certainly been worked, but it did seem rather unwise to publish the working details. I appreciate his concern. After all, you do not give a razor to a small child any more than you offer details of how to work a confidence trick or organize outright fraud. All the same, you can look at this sort of thing in other ways. For instance, if more people knew the methods which you fellows apply in order to line your pockets, they would be on their guard. Boiled down, I suppose that you could call this book a consumer service. I hope it does not rile you to see your methods described in so much excruciating detail. It has been written without any hard feelings.

Cordially,

Frederick Oughton

Chapter One

The Acorn Syndrome

Conmen should, of course, be in charge of the National Debt, the day to day rummaging in the economic affairs of the country and, in fact, any large-scale activity which involves the redistribution of wealth. The productivity growth of conmen shoots off the top of the graph paper year by year, but, as this is a comparatively harmless and bloodless crime, the police generally prefer to put it on the top shelf, and so while it is not exactly out of sight and out of mind, it is not in the same class as, say, the control of political demonstrations, traffic problems, drug peddling, burglary and murder. Yet it increases faster than any of these as far as one can estimate. The reason for the increase is that of all crimes the conman's game is the most difficult to detect. For instance, just suppose that you see an advertisement offering a bargain. You mail your cheque, but the bargain does not arrive. You send an enquiry. Silence. You write again. In the end you write to the paper in which the advertisement appeared, and by this time the bird is on the wing. Of course, to many people this is a simple, even laughable, example, because it concerns something which costs only a fiver and today a fiver is fag money. On the receiving end, the operator exists on the idea of receiving about one hundred replies and off he goes for a £500 cruise. Or perhaps he goes to another town and does it all over again. By the end of the year he has made more than £2,000. Simple.

Or, as Benjy would say: 'Dead simple.'

Benjy was small, stout, affable, shifty, generous, seldom happy, and after spending ten of the postwar years in a marriage to a girl who wanted everything, he fled. He appeared on my doorstep one hot night in search of a room and he was prepared to sleep anywhere. He paid in advance and moved in, humping a cracked black suitcase upstairs, sweating and coughing out his thanks to me. Halfway up, he slumped down on the landing and produced a bottle of beer from his overcoat pocket. Between swigs, he told me about his married life and its demands, his own inadequacy, the rottenness of civilization. All he wanted, he said, was a quiet easy life. About a week later a teenage girl moved in to help him find peace. Her name was Estelle. She brightened up my all-male household with her frequent appearances in a see-through dressing gown and a kind of Cockney cheerfulness. She was by profession a shoplifter, or heist, or keister. One day I was short of some tinned mushroom soup, so she popped out for ten minutes and returned with the soup and a couple of avocado pears. Being completely flat-chested and wearing a slack bra, she could not resist them as she came out of the corner delicatessen. She put them down very carefully, said, 'They're still warm, kiddo,' gave me a long, slow sexless wink and went back upstairs to Benjy.

Every now and then Benjy borrowed cigarettes, promising to return them with interest. Eventually he did so, and I stared hard at the parcel. 'That's a thousand fags. Last you for a bit, won't they, eh?' He laid himself down on my settee, remarking that as I was what he called 'a hard working git' I deserved my rewards. For himself, he was hard at work on his own future. 'See, it's like this. Y'know the old acorn? Grows and grows. So that's my line, acorns.'

And so it was. He collected the acorns on Hampstead Heath and in Hyde Park. He had several thousand of them in bags and sacks in his room, and any moment now it would be all systems go. His advertisement in gardening magazines provoked hundreds of ten-shilling postal orders in the first week. Few gardeners would resist the temptation to grow 'Your own exotic Japanese oaks from pedigree acorns collected by qualified plant hunters.'

But, as the CID officer told me several weeks after Benjy departed, supervising Estelle, who carried the suitcase: 'A very common confidence trick, sir, dressing something up to make it special. Clear case of misrepresentation. We've had some of his acorns down to the Royal Horticultural Society. They say they're ordinary English acorns. I'm a gardener myself and he took me in for a bit.'

The police went away and I never saw them again, but Benjy and Estelle returned from time to time to discuss their latest schemes, such as selling French letters, each one pin-pricked as a practical joke against humanity. There were dirty postcards, bought by the thousand from a salvage broker. And the buried-treasure maps of non-existent islands. By such means they became comparatively wealthy and they even had a car. They simultaneously rented at least six bedsitters. They ate and drank regularly. Benjy put on a lot of weight until he became quite porcine and apparently easy-going, but one could sense that he still had that razor brain behind the mask-like face. With me he was always relaxed.

'Still in the blood game, are you?' He always referred to my hospital work in this way. He wiped his face and started worrying about Estelle and her free and easy approach to the money which took so much earning. All that envelope opening, all that running round the accommodation addresses (5*s* a week) and, worse, all that *thinking*!

He borrowed my razor and shaved himself. 'Problems I've got. Look, my mother, she's going on about it, about me chucking my missus up. Threatening to get after me for some maintenance. My mother, she says she'll back my missus up. I ask you! No loyalty, that's her trouble.'

'You could afford to pay maintenance,' I said. 'That's the price of peace.'

'That's what you say. I'm on the dole, been on it for weeks.' He picked a match out of the ashtray and poked it down his ear. 'Wax,' he said, inspecting the blob. 'I always had wax since I was a kid. Soon as I've had six weeks on the dole, I go sick, get benefit. Then give it a rest for a week or two, then start all over again.'

He was not, he said as an afterthought, making more than £150 a week. Or it might be £200. He did not keep any books and it took time to get statements from five or six banks where he kept his money. When he went to bed at night, he pulled the blankets right over his head. Estelle slept wherever she fancied at one or another of their bed sitters. It had come down to that.

Benjy's old room was now occupied by another tenant, Mr Owen, aged and respectable, and dressed at all hours of the day and night in a black suit with a startling yellow and green tie. I assumed that he was retired and fed up with life, because he had a dusty grey look about him, as though he had filed too many papers for a succession of grinding employers and looked for too many jobs. His wife was probably dead, his children married and settled elsewhere. Yes, he was on the rubbish heap of life, I decided, and so lonely that he seldom spoke more than two words, even when he paid his rent, and I guessed that he must belong to several pen-friend clubs, because he received letters almost every day. He posted quite a few, too, hobbling slowly down the road to the postbox under the trees, where he paused, looking at the birds in the branches and whistling at them. He seemed to live on fish and chips from the fry-up round the corner. His skin had the look of uncooked batter. Gradually and imperceptibly, he began to get on my nerves, although I wanted to help him. If only he would talk. It came to the point where I started asking pointed questions, making excuses to visit his room in the evenings. In the end he snapped in my face: 'You're snooping and noseying. I pay my rent, I want my privacy. Now, what is it?'

'What's what?' I asked feebly.

'This bloody noseying.' He was quite steamed up about it. 'This poking and prying! I pay my rent—'

'Of course you do, Mr Owen.'

Something—perhaps his own professional pride—made him nudge me into his room. The door clicked shut. He lit a cigarette, and I suddenly realized that he had changed; he was much more belligerent and calculating as he eyed me up and down.

Years ago he had been a solicitor's clerk, but some money went astray and he was forced to shoulder the blame. Three years inside. He had learned a lot in prison, but mainly how to listen and think. As a result of that experience, he decided never to work again for anybody except himself. There were unlimited possibilities.

He drew hard on the cigarette. 'Yes, unlimited possibilities, that's what I thought. One thing I'd made up my mind about and it was that I'd never clock in at nine and bow and scrape and worry about my job. Ever felt like that?'

'Not particularly. I do my job and don't worry too much.'

'All I can say is you're lucky. I'd had enough. That's why I decided to become a letter writer.'

'I see,' I said, but I didn't, and I pressed him for more details, and he said: 'Letters, just letters asking for money.'

'Begging letters—' I started.

He made a contemptuous gesture. 'I'll show you.' He produced a large leather case and snapped it open. It was a portable office, full of all kinds of writing paper, a copy of the Army List, a directory of churchmen, envelopes of all sizes. He opened a ledger, placing it before my eyes long enough for me to see receipts of sums of money between £10 and £50. 'My earnings!' he swept his hand over page after page.

'It's a bit parasitic,' I started.

He was angry with me because I had presumed to judge his way of life. That night he left. No more mail came for him.

In the normal way, of course, you do not meet conmen face to face unless you happen to be a judge, or wealthy, or you are one of those people who get mentioned in the social columns, which makes you a natural target. You have to be a big fish. I was a minnow who happened to let rooms, and in the process my interest in conmen grew. This kind of preoccupation is like a hand laid lightly on your sleeve with a grip which gradually tightens. It is as well at the outset to make my own attitude quite clear, because I have an academic admiration for the ingenuity of conmen, especially when they are the architects of huge international schemes and their targets are banks, insurance companies and the leisured élite. But when ordinary people are mercilessly conned, I bridle. I have myself been done several times over the years.

Some forms of crime require a certain social climate in which to flourish, but confidence tricks will work anywhere at any time, and their patterns of operation are fairly consistent. Wherever vulgar wealth is displayed, the parasites will gather. Where greed can be tapped, the fast buck merchant will be in the offing. Because I am not a sociologist, I cannot comment very adequately on the recent rise in criminal trends, but something can be deduced from such facts as the 1968 increase of 10 per cent. In the first six months of 1969 there was a further increase of 9 per cent. The current figures, as yet not released, are probably higher. Something like 80 per cent of all crime is against property, and fraud can be included in this category. A cynical economist recently remarked that of all national industries, crime is the one which shows the most impressive rise in growth and productivity. What he failed to realize was that while the losses are in the region of £50 million a year, criminologists assert that only approximately 15 per cent of crime is actually reported and investigated. The implication is that in Britain alone rather more than six million crimes a year go unreported, and more than 50 per cent of these are fraud-orientated. During 1970 the estimated total cost of crime in Britain was more than £1,000 million. If the cost of fire damage is taken at £500 million, this means a wastage rate of 4 per cent of the gross national product. As a matter of fact, the annual growth rate of the national company is 4 per cent.

Although there is more fraud than murder, fewer police officers are trained in detection techniques in fraud than in apprehending the murderer. While human life is sacred, money is in this sense very cheap, and if the conman happens to relieve you of a few pounds, it can be replaced in most cases. Human life cannot be replaced. This is the kind of reasoning which seems to underlie the police point of view, and, as a consequence, fraud and white-collar crime continue to flourish like the green bay tree.

But what is the reason for the phenomenal increase in fraud? It is, after all, a crime which calls for a better than normal intelligence, it takes some planning, and it may require working alone. On the other hand, once you know how, it is as easy as driving a car, and it can be conducted virtually anywhere, from hotel rooms, bedsitters or by a man on the move. A prominent police officer once told me that if he did decide on a life as a conman, he would buy a car and a comfortable caravan and travel round the country, leaving his mobile home some distance away from somnolent country towns where he would make a quick killing, using some fast money scheme, and then move on. 'If I couldn't make from £7,000 to £10,000 a year out of it, I'd be a bloody duffer,' he twinkled at me. Even while this is being written a police bulletin on the radio is giving details of a conman who evidently studies the rewards offered by private individuals, and then arrives to masquerade as a police inspector, telling the victim that the stolen goods have just been recovered and can be claimed at a police station some distance away. As far as the reward is concerned, he suggests that it could be donated to a police charity, and it so happens that he is the treasurer of the area branch. The cheque is gratefully made out to bearer. Of course, by the time the victim reaches the police station to identify his property, the 'inspector' has managed to cash the cheque in a pub or through a tradesman, and that is that.

The police officer who told me how he could make a living as a conman pointed out that while every large town in the country has its own Fraud Squad of about ten men, who undergo special training, there are still great swathes of the British Isles which are virtually uncovered for the investigation of this type of offence. These include the corners of counties which are invariably inhabited by wealthy people and policed by a friendly rural officer who is quite untrained in fraud investigation. On such a case it does take time to conduct a preliminary interview, make notes, see any witnesses, and then sit down and tap out a report for his superior who, in turn, may have to go and see the victim and then finally decide to refer it to the Fraud Squad at the nearest police headquarters. This is in no way a criticism of the officers themselves but of the system, although there are signs of improvement in the formation of the regional crime squads which are not, however, designed to deal with the rapid tracing of the mobile conman, which would be too time-wasting. Whether this innovation will improve matters remains to be seen, but we should not overlook the fact that a high percentage of victims either let too much time go by before confiding to the police or are reluctant to admit their own unworldliness, and so they do not in the end report the matter at all. This may seem quaint and cowardly, but when all is said and done, who wants to admit that he has been taken for a sucker?

Perhaps I am painting too rosy a picture for future white-collar Fagins, but whichever way you look at it, you must admit that opportunities abound not only in the country areas but in London itself, where the responsibility for fraud investigation is in the hands of the City of London and Metropolitan Fraud Squad, with a staff of 100 men. It would obviously be ideal if all these men were qualified accountants and criminologists with degrees in psychology, complete with filing-cabinet brains and a penchant for running searching eyes over ledgers and files and bank statements, and they should, of course, be quick on the uptake as far as interviewing techniques are concerned. The reverse is the case. Efforts are being made to provide special training courses in London, Birmingham and Manchester, but we are still in a situation where Fraud Squad officers have to pick up their knowledge from one case to the next. When you realize that sixteen out of twenty people cannot even read and fully understand a simple company balance sheet, the same average applies to policemen, who probably have their work cut out studying for normal promotion examinations.

In London the Fraud Squad, set up in 1946, is concerned mainly with company fraud, but, equally, they investigate hundreds of small-time swindles and generally attempt to pass these on to the CID. This is not a case of passing the buck, but you have to appreciate the weight of work caused when a company is investigated, when the officers may have to remove hundreds of files and ledgers from the firm's offices. Even the contents of wastepaper baskets are dumped in bags and carefully docketed. Once it has been unloaded and stacked up at the other end, the work of examination, which may go on for months, commences with what amounts to a general audit of the books. When a firm operates from more than one office, the job becomes even more difficult. A London company with accounts manipulated by a chief accountant aided by half a dozen trainees, who did not know what was going on, had nine sets of books for branches and sub-departments, and only by auditing all of them and then comparing figures was it discovered that the cash flow had been milked at five different points. Naturally, the chief accountant, with his power boat, cabin cruiser, two houses, three cars and substantial investments in safe reliable government stock, was the man behind it.

But it is not always the most obvious man who is the architect of such a scheme. A private enquiry agent who specializes in fraud detection told me about a mail order firm with a national name but no boss who had ever been seen by members of the staff.

'A real Raymond Chandler situation. They had a warehouse and offices, all well done, and I was very impressed with it when I walked in. The chief clerk called me in and said there'd been some stock pinched and some money lifted. Usual story, I guess. He gave me a fair outline of it and said I could have a free run, and he paid me a good retainer, and left me to have a look round. I suggested he should introduce me to the staff as a new member of the firm. When I said I'd better talk to the managing director, he said he never came in. He left everything to the chief clerk and he'd been there for years. So I had to let that one go, of course, because he seemed to have the authority. Anyway, I looked round and nobbled one bloke who was knocking off garden tools and flogging them. But I didn't feel it was important. Then I was in the office one morning and there was a junior, doing the mail, sorting it out, and he said something about there being the usual lot of complaints about non-deliveries. So when he wasn't looking, I took a squint and found a file full of complaints, hundreds and hundreds of them, and I had another sniff round. It turned out that stuff was being despatched all right and a bloke in the transport firm was in on it and he was being paid to dump some of it at a warehouse a few miles away, and I found out there was a kind of shadow firm, flogging them cheap through a discount store in another town. It had been going on for months, but what I wanted to know was why? It gnawed and gnawed at me, so in the end I went to see the chief clerk and he got shirty about it, and he told me to stick to what I was paid to do. That was enough for me to get going on him, and by the time I'd examined the company registration and checked up here and there, I knew one thing, he wasn't the chief clerk, he was the managing director. That was a turn up for the book. It didn't take me long to see him and explain what I'd found out. That did him. He told me the firm was in difficulties, so he'd worked out this racket of vanishing goods, and he was fending off the customers by telling them the stuff would be replaced after the insurance was fixed up. What he was doing was getting twice the profit on the same goods, flogging them through discount stores. It was very complicated, but it worked for him. What I wanted to know was why he'd hired me. He said it was genuine enough, because one or two of the staff had been knocking things off, and he objected to it. As soon as he told me about it, he bunked off somewhere. I'd been paid, so I went, and that was the end of it, but I gave the facts to the police and left it to them.'

While many private detectives investigate a great deal of small-time fraud, some of the élite do specialize in company crime, and it is possible that the élite of the membership of the Association of British Detectives, which is the professional organization, is actually better equipped than the Fraud Squad. The situation is, after all, entirely different for the police officer and there is something vaguely ludicrous about expecting him to have an expert knowledge of accountancy, which is the key to many investigations at this level. One officer who opted out of Fraud Squad work told me: 'When I was in it, we often had to question chartered accountants, some of the top men in the profession, and you could guess what they were thinking . . . like, "Just listen to this dumb bugger, trying to understand the finer points of finance.". . . Well, what can you expect when a non-professional questions a professional? It's bound to become patronizing, and believe me it can be sheer murder, like trying to question a neuro-surgeon about the way he conducted a certain operation. But even so, there are some damned smart men in the Fraud Squad, but they've got there despite the system, not due to it. It's a job you need a flair for, like murder investigation or any other police work.'

While a dedicated Fraud Squad officer will go about his work with an almost unbelievable thoroughness, there still exists a very real danger in formulating his case, that it will be done at a level which is right over the head of the average juror, despite the fact that it is supposed to be intelligible to him. Picture the juror who has to sit through days or even weeks of cross-examination about ledger entries, high finance and transactions. A juror can be a ditch digger or a managing director, a housewife or a scientist. Put all these people together in a jury room and on the law of averages alone it is obvious that very few of them will have a clear picture of financial fraud. Anybody with a nodding acquaintance of courtroom procedure will realize that a doubtful jury will generally do the safe thing and acquit. Because this is especially true of fraud and white-collar crime, guilty men do go free. After recent City fraud cases many prominent legal brains came to the conclusion that it would be desirable to form what would in effect be a City Court with a standing panel of highly qualified accountants, directors, consultants of one kind or another and others, who would be available on a rotating basis and be paid an attractive fee for their services. But various things do go against this proposition. For one thing, it does suggest a secluded Star Chamber, a kind of holy of holies, and it could be open to abuse, taking into account that the business world is a relatively small one in which everybody knows everybody else, especially in specific trades. There is an apocryphal story about a company rigger who started so many bucket-shops that in the end one company was swindling another company, and he inevitably bankrupted himself and was saved only by organizing an internal takeover. The story may be apocryphal but it is indicative of the octopus-like structure of many companies, both legitimate and illegal, and there are many dangers in this kind of financial incest which lends itself to abuse. On the face of it, the notion of a select City Court to mete out special justice is unacceptable in Britain, although the Americans tackled the problem many years ago, setting up Better Business Commissions on an inter-state basis with quasi-legal powers, and in some cases it is the Commission itself which prepares the case for the prosecution, using its own staff of attorneys. In effect, this organization does the job which, in Britain, is tackled by the Fraud Squad, and once again we are driven to the conclusion that the British pattern, while good of its kind, lacks equipment and men. It is the weakness of British investigation facilities and the law which suggests that, of all crime, fraud is still the easiest to perpetrate and, let it be whispered, the easiest in which to avoid prosecution. Some of the wealthiest people in the world are not Greek shipowners or American oilmen but mobile con-men, their real identities and background quite unknown not only to the public but to the police themselves. While some live quietly behind their dark glasses, others openly declare themselves to be of independent means. Practically all of them are friendly, generous and they hate poverty. One sweaty summer afternoon in Wimbledon, I sat talking to a highly qualified barrister who went now and then to the kitchen to see how a large piece of meat was faring in the oven. While it was hissing and spitting in the background, we concentrated on the malt whisky, and he meandered through details of his latest deal. Acting on behalf of one of the most respected British companies, he had just sold several hundred tractors to the Chinese Communist government. All of them were defective. It was something to do with the gearbox. His commission was £15,500 in a single cheque, which now lay slightly sodden on the table between the glasses and the bottles. Several months later, when the Chinese technical advisers complained about the tractors, he flew over and sold them one million pounds' worth of spare parts to repair the tractors. This time there was another commission cheque for all his trouble, and he and his wife went to live quietly abroad. Naturally, fraud on this scale does not warrant legal action. It is too damned big to prosecute, as the perpetrator was at pains to point out to me when I said that it was hard cheese on the Communists.

From what has been said already, it would appear that most fraud and white-collar crime is beyond the understanding of Mr Ordinary Man. This is not exactly so, especially when you appreciate the fact that all it amounts to is common theft and the Board of Trade acts as the public watchdog for company frauds. No matter how complicated a crime seems to be, it should be possible to summarize it in a single short paragraph. This idea is drummed into the head of every Fraud Squad officer who, in the midst of a morass of figures, may begin to wonder what the hell the case is all about. So ravelled are some cases that this little schoolroom exercise must be done several times by all the officers working on the same case. It is surprising how these individual summaries may differ. During this phase of the investigation the purpose is to frame a case for presentation to the Director of Public Prosecutions who is, at the time of writing,

Sir Norman Skelhorne, Q.C. The DPP is among the faceless men of the law, but he is one of the most powerful, for it is he who finally decides whether there is a case to answer. Exactly how he accomplishes this when considering a case which may eventually figure as Regina versus the criminal where fraud is concerned is very much shrouded in secrecy, but it can safely be said that the DPP's department certainly does not consist of Sir Norman and a super-secretary who somehow decide whether Mr X has been sufficiently naughty to warrant socking him with a summons. Cases which are referred to the DPP must pass through an elaborate filtration system until they finally reach the yes/no stage and the DPP himself makes the decision. Staging a trial for fraud is not undertaken too lightly in view of the fact that it can cost £1,000 or more a day out of the public purse. Sir Norman and his cadre are therefore faced with a number of knotty problems while being conscious that such a trial can be put on only when it is clear that the law has been broken and a case must therefore be brought in the public interest. It can work the other way round, of course, because if the DPP and his advisers are not satisfied with the police contention that the law has been broken, the papers are returned, and that, in many instances, is that, to the chagrin of officers who may have spent months working it all out. Just because the police decide to proceed with a case of this kind, it does not mean that the judiciary will agree, which is just as well. More than one-third of cases put up to the DPP are rejected, and these are all within the fraud category, and it is not entirely unknown for the DPP's office to indulge in some polite horse trading to try and streamline the proceedings provided a case is brought. The police may have a particular interest in doing some trickster or other, but the DPP's office will be dispassionate in its evaluation of the chances of the trial. Police charges may have to be modified and some dropped while others are increased, but it seems that in many cases the DPP is more interested in saving public money by adopting measures to shorten a trial instead of laying it on thick and spending more time than is necessary in the courtroom. There naturally has to be a feedback and the accused must be consulted through his solicitor. Putting it candidly, he is propositioned. A quick trial and a short term in prison or a long trial and longer in prison . . . was there ever a conman unwilling to make a bargain?

Clearly, there is a certain amount of dissatisfaction in the way that the DPP's office stands in relation to the police and, equally clearly, there is a need to improve the Fraud Squad system, primarily in London but also throughout Britain. There is now far more fraud than ever before. The Fraud Squad, formed in March 1946 under the leadership of Chief Superintendent Thorp, dealt with 290 cases in the first twelve months. Since that time the number of cases has increased so that it is today a tidal wave, and the official policy for today is that all fraud should be nipped in the bud rather than be allowed to go on. One former officer said: 'There was a firm which just sprang up and it managed to get about £200 a day out of the public. There isn't much point telling you how it was done—you might have a go at it yourself!—but we got to know about it early on. They'd had a couple of thousand out of people and we got a list of the suckers together. I stepped round and put the fear of Christ into the big chap, and when I told him we wouldn't take it any further if he sent all the money back otherwise he would get ten years—well, he agreed. So I said I'd be round next day and he could start writing those cheques, and in the meantime I had a quiet word with his bank manager to make sure he'd got the funds. It was all over in a couple of days. It's really a matter of looking at a bloke like that with a gimlet eye and showing him you can lean on him. You've only got to mention the word misrepresentation and they jump quick enough.'

Before we proceed it may be of interest to know how much the Director of Public Prosecutions is paid. The figure is £7,500 a year. The deputy director receives £5,335, the assistant directors £3,735 to £4,585, the assistant solicitors £3,733 to £4,585, the senior legal assistants £2,621 to £3,585, the legal assistants £1,639 to £2,516 and the senior executive officer £2,062 to £2,496. A good bunco artist can make two or three times more than any of these. And he does not have to get there at nine a.m. or pay income tax. Untramelled by the need to keep up appearances beyond the bounds of duty, he can change his name and depart. For the conman the loopholes are many. For instance, you can use any name you wish and you can change your name at will and at any time without any legal formalities or expense.

Personal identity is, however, the least of it. The biggest anomaly is in the fact that a limited liability company can be set up and registered for as little as £25, and it is the company itself which provides a measure of protection for the conman.

There are firms which will sell you a ready-made company with no more formality than your signature on a cheque in return for the company documents. Literally anybody of legal age can become a company director within a couple of weeks, and what you do with your company is up to you. You can raise credit, you can trade in goods, or you may prefer merely to have your company for a simple purpose, such as income tax. Thousands of people bought companies for themselves when the Inland Revenue put the squeeze on. After all, a company director has expenses, and expenses are to some extent tax deductible. Almost overnight several thousand people became amateur conmen. Even today an estimated £150 million of income tax goes unpaid every year, much of it due to the operations of ghostly companies which have misty assets but huge expenses and overheads. Most of them operate three years in arrears, and so crushing is the amount of work within the Inland Revenue that there is practically no hope of catching up with the dodgers.

For the conman there are great advantages in having a company to call his own, and the first one is undobutedly sheer status. Naïve as we are, we still have an image of the company director as a man of character and substance. Granted the right environment, the conman-company director can sell shares in his company on the strength of a beautiful letterhead, a business card, perhaps a brochure or two. These are the usual trappings, the hooks for the poor sucker fish. The second asset is the ability to raise credit. According to the police, credit is one of the bugbears of the age, and to the conman it is generally the basis of fraud, especially where companies are concerned. We cannot expect the system to change, and it is perfectly obvious that business itself cannot exist without various forms of credit. The conman with his ghostly company, or the crooked consortium which is run by several tricksters, know how to misuse methods of raising credit. A cheque is itself a form of credit note and, since it takes three or four days to clear a cheque, it follows that the number of rubberized cheques is always on the increase, and practically all the banks daily RD cheques. It has become routine, despite the fact that it is an offence to issue a cheque when you know that insufficient funds exist to meet it. A crooked company can pledge its credit, obtain goods which it can sell, and by this means raise cash, which is used for various other purposes.

The third asset of having a company is the knowledge that the Department of Trade will take a considerable time when frauds are extremely complicated. In some cases a generation of civil servants can retire and the case be passed on to the younger newcomers. Unlike vice, murder and other kinds of crime, fraud is a nebulous thing which can bounce back and forth, presenting tremendous difficulties for the investigating officers, who have very limited powers, and while they may know what the crime is, or was, they must find out precisely how it was perpetrated. The big conmen are somewhat brainier than the authorities, and this is a fact which should be acknowledged. What the investigating officer does know is that he will find it hard to pinpoint the person who planned it and the person who actually executed it. Some finer points of law have to be grappled with, because up to comparatively recently a business corporation stood outside the law on the hypothesis that a corporation was not a person, and it could not be indicted as such. This was Roman Law. In more recent times it has become obvious that dangers do exist and, as things now stand, a company can be indicted in the company name and it can be fined as a company. There are variations on this theme, but what it does mean in the broadest terms is that an unscrupulous operator can shelter behind a company name, pay a fine when detected, and then start up elsewhere to repeat the same profitable trick all over again. The conman's first aim is to go on doing this for as long as possible, all the time piling money into any number of bank accounts or investments. If he spends enough time preparing for the killing by studying company law and finding loopholes and creating his front, it is highly unlikely that he will ever go to prison, despite Section 188 of the Companies Act, which prevents a convicted person from setting up again for five years. The conman operating at this level who really knows his stuff is virtually fireproof. As an American conman, Joseph Weil, once said: 'Perhaps the most important of all my qualifications was a good knowledge of the law. . . . Over the years, I have seen many new laws passed —some of them restricting the freedom of the individual. No doubt I was the inspiration for some of these statutes.'

It is odd that criminologists have not paid more attention to fraud and white-collar crime, and those who have attempted to dissect it have not reached agreement as to the reasons for this type of offence. Actually, it is quite simple, and the answer can be dropped neatly into a nutshell, because the reason is common avarice or plain greed. Towards the end of this chapter I shall have more to say about this. In the meantime, we are still examining the acorn syndrome of the growth of fraud and trickery in our own time.

The economic climate of industry has brought forth its own little monster, and this is called industrial espionage, which, in turn, has created a new kind of operator. He is employed by a company behind which are the faceless men who represent a very real danger to the economic system, because they are parasitic, and far from being directly interested in the acquisition, their attention is focused on information. During the discussion of a paper on 'Industrial Secrets and Crime', read to the Royal Society of Arts in December 1969, Mr A. E. Osborne said: 'We are talking as if British industry is being constantly sinned against, but in fact it is just as guilty of espionage as any other European country. The other day I was talking to a representative of a nameless, very major, chemical company and I asked what they would do if an industrial spy produced a certain photograph of new plant being laid by a competitor in Europe. The answer (from a very high official) was "If he came in through the front door we should show him out smartly. If he came in through the back, that would be another question".'

Commercial spying carefully selects and develops its operators on an international scale, and every now and then I run into one of the front-line troops, Jimmy. Aged 43, he is ostensibly a consultant who is particularly well known in one branch of industry for his ability to cure sick companies and restore them to profitability. In his other role he is a ruthless, unabashed liar who trades boardroom secrets. In this respect he is in direct contravention of the ethical code of the Management Consultants Association. Far from being unobtrusive and ordinary looking, he is a jet setter, always back from somewhere or off to America or Hong Kong, a silk-suited symbol with a walletful of credit cards and lunch always at the nearest Hilton, which he calls his snack bar. Yet the same man will instantly drop his cigar and champagne routine and take a remarkably menial job in a firm for the sake of obtaining certain information which cannot be acquired in any other way. He uses forged testimonials and a ready-made background, and in a creased suit and down-at-heel shoes he is capable of looking like a badly paid clerk.

The agitation over industrial spying has been smouldering for several years, and despite counter-espionage measures which are offered by national security firms and a certain number of self-employed security agents, industrial secrets and confidential information worth millions of pounds changes hands every year. Industrial counter-espionage is a peculiar game. It is not simply a matter of seeing that trade secrets are handled only by authorized personnel who have been screened to the nth degree but of some front-line fighting which may itself involve using illegal methods. In this sense, the counter-espionage man is in the battleground between industry and the people who are trying to get at it. The consolation is that rewards are high. A good agent will start thinking in terms of annual income of more than £5,000.

Firms like I.C.I., Shell, and many others have elaborate internal security systems, but however good these are, it is not unusual to discover too late that details of a new process have leaked across the Atlantic or as far afield as Hong Kong, which is one of the great trafficking markets for material of this sort. Provided that a suitably qualified person can be found and planted, no secrets are entirely safe, and one of the ploys of the counter-espionage agent is seeing to it that the wrong secrets, which seem genuine, are the ones which are stolen. Although this might at first seem to be plain theft, it is not necessarily the case. Some weeks ago I attended a meeting to discuss this very point, and it transpired that from the legal point of view the most an industrial spy could expect was a charge of theft if he removed a sheet of paper from a file and took it off the premises of its owner. If he did this while in the employ of the firm but returned to the premises after working hours, he could be charged with trespass. Nowadays it would be a naïve operator who would risk this. He uses the office copier and replaces the original in the file within seconds of removing it. In the Soviet Union copying machines and duplicators are regarded as military equipment, but in the average business premises in the West practically everybody has access to them. Jimmy once showed me a copying machine which fitted into his briefcase and still left room for papers. And there is always the vest-pocket camera. Nowadays most industrial spies use the slim Minox, which costs only £80. The employers and their associations and organizations are still looking into the state of the law, and it would seem that the element of fraud enters into it when the spy lands the job by pretending to be something other than what he actually is, although few firms would try to charge a man on this basis. If forged references are discovered, however, a charge could be made which carries a maximum sentence of seven years.

Industrial espionage is not simply a matter of a man getting a job in a factory or office. There are employment and executive placement agencies. In this rarified form of fraud an elaborate set-up is used. The picture must look right all the way down the line. Midway stands the placement bureau. At a time when dozens of executive placement agencies are found in London alone, the new and deliberately unobtrusive one will pass muster. They have to look respectable and they must fit into the executive picture. The reputable ones do have their own association to ensure that members conform to the highest standards. In London they are licensed annually and they are open to inspection. But outside this respectable milieu are the shiny sharp agencies which mushroom and get round the regulations by calling themselves something else. They are scheduled to live for a limited period, the intention being to present a front so that they can place their smart young, or even middle-aged, men in jobs in the firms where information is waiting to be picked up for the client who is waiting in the background. They somehow manage to bring their services to the notice of the target firm, and this is done by mailing out attractive brochures, which stress the low fees to the employer, undercutting other agencies. Every artifice of salesmanship is employed, culminating in a call on the personnel manager. It may take months or weeks, but it generally works. From there it is only a matter of time before the candidate is in. The system seems to work on gullibility—the gullibility of the personnel manager, and more than one operator in this field has emphasized that many personnel executives are extremely lazy and only too glad to let the outside agency with an understanding of his needs wade through all the tedious preliminary interviews. As Jimmy said: 'Plan it right, get to know the personnel manager, study his weaknesses, and you can practically guarantee to get a man in there sooner or later.' This is not necessary a calumny on personnel managers as a class, it is simply a fact of business life. In one case, when no openings could be found in the management echelon, Jimmy's organization discovered that a position for a printroom manager existed in a department where confidential documents were photocopied by the dozen. As it turned out, it could not have been a better position for an industrial spy, because he was able to help himself to several copies of everything that passed through his hands, and in no time he had a dossier several inches thick which, in due course, he took out of the building in a plain envelope and posted to a Continental address. For six months of leisurely work the firm paid him £22 a week, but for the collection of the documents he received a fee of £3,000. When the time was right, he gave in his notice and he and the firm parted on good terms.

Fraud of this kind often goes entirely unsuspected, and a firm may never realize that it has been the victim of a carefully planned operation to wrest its inner secrets away for study by the opposition or even a consortium of interests which will, in due course, sell the information. Even the biggest companies are not completely disinterested in acquiring information when it is offered at the right price.

The more bland and innocent-seeming the front which is presented to the world, the more suspicious one may feel after some idea of the *modus operandi* has been studied. Counter-espionage operators are particularly interested in the *modus operandi* which fits into the following framework, for it has many variations: first, get your information; second, use it or sell it as quickly as possible, especially if it is of a technical nature, because it may date; third, make sure there is no feedback, no betrayal. These three steps apply to the smallest firm or the biggest government, and I would like to cite two instances of how it works in practice.

The first one concerns publishing and the book-production industry. In London this is, in comparison with other industries, a fairly small parish-pump affair with several hundred publishing houses which among them produce more than 35,000 titles a year, ranging from cheap handbooks to weighty scientific tomes costing nearly £70 a copy. Although it is not big in terms of industrial size, and very few publishers actually own their production facilities, the export record is impressive, and profitability varies from one firm to another. Although it is said to be a profession for gentlemen, the undercover competition is surprising savage. Ideas for books are common, but good ideas are at a premium. And for present purposes that is probably all you need to know about the publishing industry. It was also the extent of his knowledge when a former army officer moved in. Quite by chance, he discovered that some publishers will often spend large sums of money researching the viability of a proposed book by consulting their sales representatives, by paying fees to freelance consultants and sometimes by crossing the Atlantic to fix up a cost-sharing deal, also by trying to arrange pre-publication deals for paperback and other rights in several foreign markets. This applies mainly to non-fiction books, from biographies to textbooks of various kinds. He also knew that Britain contained several dozen talented hack writers, who in return for a cheque of the right size and colour could put their pens to any subject at the drop of a hat. In deference to hack writers generally, it should be made quite plain that these gifted creators have the edge over their more specialized brothers, who are able to write on relatively few subjects. If hacks do not achieve fame, their bank balances are generally in a very healthy condition.

The man to whom I have referred discovered that it took between nine and twelve months to publish a book. He figured that if he could get to know the plans of publishers in regard to fast-selling technical and general interest books, he could employ hack writers to produce books with the same title (there is no copyright on titles) within three months, use a fast-moving printer and binder, and then put them on the market. The problem of how to discover publishers' future plans was solved quite easily. All he did was consult advance publicity at the shop of a friendly bookseller, and in time he organized a cover address and circularized all publishers, asking for catalogues and news of new books.

It may sound incredible, but this piracy paid off. He built up an impressive list of quick-selling textbooks, reference works and sheer ephemera by picking the brains of others.

That was small stuff. Now for the big one, which brings us up to date.

This concerns a government. The country is a major power with industrial interests throughout the world. It would be unwise to name the colossus, because it could impair diplomatic relations.

Many industries have political links, especially when military contracts are involved and public money is being spent. In this sense it should be realized that many industries are run by the government, although the connection is generally obscure to all except a few economists and business analysts.

The government in question runs commercial bureaux in their embassies throughout the world, and they are staffed by technologists, professional commercial intelligence officers and 'co-ordinators'. It might seem that between them these highly trained and qualified men could effectively handle all the probing, collecting and evaluating, but this is far from being the case, because they employ others and pay them so well that while the purpose of any particular exercise might not be revealed in its entirety, we can assume that the fees are sufficiently adequate to keep everybody happy. In London no more than four organizations exist to service the embassy.

It works like this.

The commercial department is alerted by the 'head office' back home regarding a requirement, which can concern literally any branch of applied technology from underwater X-ray photography to synthetic metal coating. Many of the subjects are far beyond the understanding of an industrial technologist, and only a handful of men have enough brainpower to know much about them. They are retained by the handful of organizations which tender for the job. The requirements, or brief, are shown on a single foolscap page, often badly duplicated and not showing the source of origin. All the embassy wants is the price or fee. Sufficient to say that a detailed report, or study, running to perhaps 100 pages may warrant a fee of between £1,500 and £5,000. A bigger one can cost up to £10,000 and take more than eighteen months to complete.

Once the organization has the contract in the bag, it utilizes an associated company to conduct the initial fact-finding work. In many cases a front organization is set up for the purpose and an office suite is taken in a business area. A special company may be registered and some dummy advertisements inserted in the relevant trade journals to condition people who may be approached later to the idea of the firm's existence. Promotional literature may be printed. In other words, a paper edifice is built and it will look remarkably solid. This is image-making, because in this trade the image is all-important.

Here is the system.

Assuming that the focus of the study is underwater photography, the 'front' firm will contain the specialist who has been brought in to compile the report. He is one of the few men who will know precisely what is wanted. He may have one or two assistants and they will be temporary senior secretaries, but none of them will know anything about the exercise. They will be told that the firm is in export/import or some such nebulous line of business. They will be well paid but not to any extravagant degree.

The next stage is to collect primary information. Nothing is more simple. There are trade directories which cover absolutely every industry, from missiles to electronic counting devices. One directory alone covers the entire field of electronics. Submarine photography is a fairly simple subject, and part of it is allied to electronics. The front firm now consults the relevant directory and sends letters off to every company in the business, asking for catalogues, lists, descriptive manuals and so on. It may send out another letter, posing a number of interesting questions and implying that a substantial order may be in the offing. In con-man's language, this is the 'come-on' or 'taster', in plain language it is the bait. Any firm worth its salt will naturally prick up its ears at the hint of a major sale.

As a result of the come-on a pile of mail arrives, and it is sorted, classified and examined, after which it is fitted into the framework of the report, giving the man in charge a fairly good picture of the industry and the product. He spends a great deal of time absorbing the information, trying to find out ways and means of probing more deeply. Almost all these projects have one object, to find out the drift of research and to get to know what kind of innovations, improvements and entirely new products are in the pipeline. Representatives of firms are invited to call. In this area of industry the representative is generally a highly qualified man, not just a salesman. They call at the office under the impression that they may be able to clinch a major sale or, at least, fertilize the ground for one to be made in future. Although they may be technically qualified, they are sales orientated. A salesman is a vulnerable person, he has his own weaknesses, and he will often say rather more than he intends once some kind of relationship in the form of lunch or drinks has been created. In the early stages, he will enlarge on the catalogue text, but clever questioning can bring out far more. In the case of the submarine camera there may be a demand for detailed data on shutter, electronic control system, lens. It is simple to fabricate questions to floor the average technical sales representative to a point where he will want to refer back to his office. This will not satisfy the customer, who will pile on questions until nothing short of a visit to the firm and a discussion with designer, technologists and other key personnel will meet the bill. For the sake of a big order, anything!

A highly skilled man knows which questions to ask and he knows how to guide boffins to the point where they reveal more than they should. A tour of the research and development laboratories and development workshops, the design office and production lines can also be useful.

By the time this process has been remorselessly repeated until every possible company connected with the product has been put under the magnifying glass, a composite picture will have been assembled. There are various ancillary aids which can be used, such as professional organizations, the editorial staffs of specialist trade and technical departments and even departments of the British government, such as the Department of Trade, which is generally profuse in helping all who need information.

What of the final phase? It is quite straightforward. The operator writes his report. A copy is typed by a girl who does not understand a single word of it. The material is then checked and sent to a printer. Copies are then bound and sent to the embassy. There may or may not be a meeting between the author and the embassy official in charge of the project to discuss one or two minor points. The copies are then packed and despatched to 'head office' after which the final settlement is made.

This is no more shocking than other forms of commercial spying, and the fact that it is done at government level makes no difference to the fact that it is still in the shadowland of espionage.

The top men in this game can make up to £125,000 a year, but in a poor year it will drop to about £50,000. What you have to bear in mind is that after a prolonged course of study at university followed by a legitimate career in industry covering fifteen to twenty years and the accompanying wear and tear on the nervous system, with a tarnished golden handshake at the age of 45 as a result of merger or takeover, a highly qualified man will realize how slender is the chance of getting another well-paid position. This is a common story among those who have gravitated into this kind of work. Not that they regret it any more than the goldbrick artist or cardsharp regrets his way of life. The difference is that the industrial conman need have no fear of receiving a call from the Fraud Squad. After all, they do not speak his language.

Social reformers and others who believe that civilization should be crime-free are faced with insuperable difficulties when it comes to fraud and white-collar crime. They may say that murder can be virtually stamped out if sufficiently harsh deterrents are applied; sex offenders can be referred to clinics; armed robbery can be eradicated if certain precautions are taken. But fraud and white-collar crime is a beast of another colour. Significantly enough, it is found only in capitalist societies, although general dishonesty is itself international and even the bosses of the Soviet agricultural communes have been known to falsify their returns. The habit of getting something for nothing starts very early on in life. During 1969 the Surrey Research Centre of the London School of Economics and Political Science under the direction of Dr W. A. Belsen announced that in one survey 89 per cent of London boys in the 13–16-year age group said that they had at some time kept things which they had found. 63 per cent admitted stealing school property. 51 per cent said that they had stolen money.

The 1968 Criminal Statistics show that just about one-quarter of all indictable offences were committed by young people up to the age of 17 years, and 25,000 by offenders under the age of 14 years.

If this were a weighty sociological treatise—which it isn't—we could look more deeply into the reasons for these startling figures, but if some degree of understanding is needed, one need only look through the popular newspapers. Where affluence was once the province of certain classes, we are now in a position where everybody wants as much as he can get, the old idea of having to work for it being quite dead. Low earning power is felt to be a drawback, even a stigma, and the constant announcements of pay increases for some classes inflames other classes. At this point the low-earning sufferer may look around for ways and means of augmenting his income, whether by stirring it up in the union or by pilfering from his firm. One thing leads to another. First, a few tools disappear, then there is a lull, followed by something big being stolen. In a South Wales factory a huge drum of conductor cable was removed without trace. The phenomenon of this situation is that pilfering escalates, even when security is tightened or increased, by which time the whole business becomes a game in which the aim is to steal more and outwit the security force at the same time.

Forecasting on the basis of past and present crime figures, McClintoch and Avison, the criminologists, predict that 8 per cent of women and 31 per cent of men will be convicted of a standard offence during their lifetimes. The estimates include the police themselves.

There is a strong temptation to explore this theme further. A perceptive investigator of the social and industrial structure finds a disturbing state of affairs. While the man on the factory floor is busy pinching tools and raw materials, at director level in the same firm some equally odd things are going on. The firm's accounts are fixed. Claims for government subsidies for new and non-existent machinery are made and paid. Any tightening up of government supervision lends zest to the game. The individual directors are at it, too. They have tame accountants to fiddle their tax returns. The firm itself may have an overdraft of £1 million or more. It operates fixed or floating expenses, it supplies company cars and charges these against depreciation. Salesmen use the same cars for private hire work. . . .

But rather than theorizing, we should be practical and start mingling with a class of criminals who would, given the chance, be astute politicians and business men. It is, however, debatable whether politicians and business men could make the grade in the opulent twilight land of this type of crime.

Chapter Two

Fraud as a Business

To start thinking in terms of fraud you must first have a penchant for fraud. You have to believe in it and, contrary to what some people might think, you need not be a failure to start with. Conmen work incredibly hard while they are actually operating. They have to, because they must maintain a believable front. It is a nerve-racking life which carries considerable rewards. If they work alone, then it is an even harder life. If they are married and the wife knows how they make money, it is not unusual for the woman to have a belief in this sort of career. Like Clever Dick.

It started in the House of Commons with an MP packing his briefcase with letters and files. He was in a hurry because he wanted to catch the train home to his constituency and he had very little time in hand. Any delay would mean getting the later train, trying to get some rest in the corner of the carriage for a few hours and making spasmodic attempts to read the letters and annotate them for reply. The life of an MP was not exactly as he had imagined it would be, and while he had created a fair record for himself in the House, he was conscious of the fact that he was swamped. To understand his position it is necessary to know that he did not belong to one of the major political parties. He was elected by a fluke majority, having been interested in their ideals for years. It so happened that the contentions of the majority suited the unrest in a depressed area, and so he was elected. If political labels must be used, you could call him an independent reactionary. He had his own business, but it was not the one for which he had been trained in the first place. He was a likeable, calm sort of fellow. In his own party there were mixed feelings about his parliamentary performance. Politicians are not intellectual giants, and Westminster is nothing more than a large committee, a bigger version of the parish council.

He was lucky to catch the train and jumped into a first-class compartment as it was pulling out. The other occupant had some papers spread out. He made room for the MP. 'I'm sorry—'

'Don't worry. I was just in time.'

They eyed each other, as men do, and they saw two lounge suits and two briefcases. Men are not very perceptive in such cases. On a railway journey there is no need to be, because it will be over and done with in a few hours. However, if you have a public face, you must expect to be recognized. Clever Dick, the other man, instantly struck up a conversation. The MP swallowed a vague annoyance which he always experienced when people would not leave him alone, and cautiously acknowledged his own identity. At any moment the fellow would be off on his hobby horse, suggesting that it was time the government dealt with this, that or t'other, and perhaps a Question could be asked. Surprisingly, nothing of the sort was said. For the first twenty miles it was simply idle conversation. Clever Dick mentioned that he had been to town to see an exhibition of machinery because he was thinking of re-equipping his works. He was, he said, in printing.

Another few miles passed. Dinner was being served. Clever Dick suggested that they share a table. The MP might like to be his guest. Over the food, the wine and the weskit buttons the conversation eased slightly. The MP became interested in the printing industry and its problems. Clever Dick seemed to be an intelligent fellow. His main difficulty was, he said, keeping all the machines fully employed. As he had come up the hard way via an apprenticeship he knew the ins and outs of it all. He stirred his coffee with a businesslike vigour. 'The biggest—ah—shall I say satisfaction I ever had was in going back to buy up the very firm where I served my apprenticeship.' He was in a reflective mood. 'Yes, very satisfying, that was.'

You are either a sucker for success stories or else you take them with a pinch of salt. Every self-made man must have either a mean streak or a fat legacy behind him. Effort without assets is unrealistic as an ingredient of success. Yet the MP was persuaded that his dinner companion was in the Samuel Smiles class, a walking example of Smiles' contention that hard work must pay off.

The train clattered on and had covered most of its journey

before the MP happened to mention that one of these days his party must think about putting their little news sheet on a better basis. It had always lacked a guiding hand, it started and stopped because nobody wanted to write the articles and supervise printing.

Clever Dick was on to this at once and soon dug out the fact that the trouble was a lack of co-ordination. At best the news sheet was simply a part-time job for a member of the party, and it always had the disadvantage of looking like a parish magazine at a time when every other political party could afford to employ bright young public relations people to produce propaganda papers which claimed public attention. Some of them even made money. The trouble was a lack of funds, the MP cautiously admitted. His party was far from wealthy and it was unlikely that a benefactor could be found to put money into the news sheet. Clever Dick pointed out that there were more ways of getting over a fence than jumping. The conversation suddenly took on a more urgent note, steered astutely by Clever Dick, who pointed out that it was a fortunate meeting in view of his own need for the full use of his printing machines and the MP's party needing a helping hand with the news sheet. Two needs could imply a mutually satisfactory solution, eh? Clever Dick beamed encouragingly. The MP could do no more than suggest that they discuss it at greater length some time in the future. While he was agreeably surprised by Clever Dick's acumen, he was still slightly adrift when it came to talking about converting a simple news sheet into a mass-circulation newspaper for a great chunk of the British Isles. But Clever Dick certainly seemed to know what he was talking about and he radiated confidence that it could be done. He would, he said generously, be willing to install a high-speed rotary printing press in due course. It could be ordered from Germany. Not only that, if the party gave him a free hand on the business side, he would make the paper into a viable proposition. Just think of it, a weekly eight-page paper in which the party could promote its policies without any difficulty at all!

As soon as the MP got home, he phoned the party secretary and mentioned the invigorating discussion on the train. Perhaps they could meet and talk about it? To understand the well-nigh incredible events which followed, it is necessary to know more about the party secretary. He had at one time been a bank worker and was reputed to know a great deal about finance and the manipulation of money. During his long term as full-time secretary of the party he had used a firm strategem to hold his position in the face of other contenders. His dedication to the party was absolute and uncompromising, and he had for many years resisted the infiltration of younger men into positions of power, although he was now fighting a losing battle. Recent months had seen the arrival of a sharp, frank-speaking university don, who was appointed assistant secretary in a milieu which had up to now been the province of middle-aged and elderly theorists. The sparks had been flying. The secretary knew that sooner or later he must produce a rabbit out of the hat to make his position more secure for the few remaining years until his retirement. This was a golden chance to do so, and it would show the young men that it took men of maturity to devise big schemes for the rejuvenation of the party.

'I think we should have a meeting,' he suggested to the MP.

The climate of fraud must be akin to that of a greenhouse where orchids are grown. It must be hot and steamy, it must have rich compost beds of speculation and hope. Fraud depends for its success on hope. A fly on the wall of the room where Clever Dick met the politicos during the next few days would have noticed the zeal which shone in the eyes of all three. Dedication and enthusiasm were in the air, but for different reasons. When they came down to earth again it was the party secretary who had some misgivings. 'But how much money will be needed?'

They both looked at Clever Dick and the atmosphere in the small back room of politicos seemed to thicken. He said that in the ordinary way he would himself 'divert' some of his own capital, but it happened to be tied up in his plans for expansion, investments and so on. As their faces dropped, he hurried on to assure them that he proposed putting a most valuable something into the project. It was called experience, a whole lifetime of expertise, and without it, he emphasized, the scheme could hardly get off the ground.

'But what would the value of this experience amount to?' the secretary enquired patiently. 'The real cash value?' He sat there, pencil over pad, waiting for the answer.

'At least £5,000 a year.' Clever Dick looked confident. 'I mean, supposing I were to take a job and use my experience in this type of job, I wouldn't do it for less than £5,000 a year.'

The MP interrupted. 'It's a serious consideration. The party would have to pay something like that to a qualified business manager to run the sort of paper we are talking about.'

The £5,000 was noted as a 'donation of services'. Any man who was apparently prepared to give that much time and the fruits of his experience must obviously be treated with respect.

'Now, what about the rest of the assets?' The MP looked hopefully from one to the other.

The secretary was still unsure how things were going. 'Well, nothing really. The existing news sheet—is that worth anything?'

Clever Dick jumped straight in. 'Of course it is. It's a foundation we can build on. Let's put an arbitrary value on it—say £2,500.'

They were now creeping towards the crunch, the point where real money would have to be discussed. Needless to say, it was Clever Dick who forced the issue. Cash to cover the first two years would have to be raised, he said, and as this was a party newspaper, the readers could be the shareholders. The MP smiled sadly. The party members were not wealthy, they were just ordinary people. The younger element could scarcely afford membership fees. Of course, they did have a kind of charity day once a year and this generally brought in £20,000, but it was always spoken for long in advance. As he was speaking, the secretary brought out a membership list of several thousand names and passed it over. Clever Dick riffled through it and did a quick sum. What about a nominal one pound per member with the option to give more?

'On a loan basis?' the MP queried.

'Or an outright gift, a donation.' Clever Dick was still sure of himself. 'I'll make your paper into a profitable and going concern. Of course, you political chaps—well, let's just say I'll make it into a viable proposition.' His listeners were not quite sure what viable meant in this context but they let it pass. 'So . . . what about it?'

'Naturally, we'll have to put it before the committee,' the secretary said cautiously.

'Of course, of course, but don't leave it too long. I have my own business to look after, you know.' Clever Dick called for three cups of tea.

Several meetings later it was decided on the suggestion of the secretary to float a debenture plan to see how the members of the party responded. A debenture is a sealed bond of corporation or company acknowledging a sum on which interest is due till the principal is repaid, and it applies especially to fixed interest which constitutes a prior charge on assets. Arranging it gave the secretary a lot of work. He framed the letter, consulted the party solicitors and finally posted copies to every single member of the party. Up to this point Clever Dick had done very little except attend meetings and supply a few inflated biographical details about himself to enable the secretary to promote confidence. In the circular letter about the debenture scheme it was pointed out that he had a deep and abiding interest in the region, and he also said that he was the proprietor of an advertising enterprise elsewhere in the country. He did not, of course, mention the fact that it was on its last legs.

Some days later the response was apparent. Once the financial tap was turned on, there was no stopping it. At the end of a few weeks £12,500 had been sent or pledged to the secretary. The idea of having a full-size newspaper to promote the cause apparently attracted everybody. Clever Dick said that it would be enough to make a start.

Now comes the really incredible part of it. When Clever Dick suggested that all the money be transferred to him, the MP and the party secretary agreed, especially when they were told that it would be deposited in an investment company. As soon as they agreed, Clever Dick formed the company with himself and his wife as directors with the qualified accountant who tended Clever Dick's other enterprises. The sum of £12,500 now rested in an account to which only Clever Dick had access because he was the sole signatory to cheques, the very first one being for £2,500 in favour of his leaking business affairs. It was the start of the familiar game of robbing Peter to pay Paul. This did not come out until much later.

No particular official of the party had been appointed to oversee the use of the funds, and, sensing that this might be a good thing for various reasons, Clever Dick himself suggested it to the secretary. The only available person was a graduate who had worked at party HQ, a likeable, ingenuous youth who was only too glad to have the title of Executive Editor of the newspaper and a few pounds a week. It was agreed that his name should head the enterprise, because he was, at least, a party member. Clever Dick himself never joined. He said that it would look too much like currying favour.

In his own neighbourhood an odd rumour now started circulating to the effect that Clever Dick was, in fact, a millionaire.

It is relatively easy to start this kind of rumour. Local tradesmen who had not been paid for weeks became less pressing. If Clever Dick was good for a million, their bills could be paid any old time, and he was, they agreed, a very good customer. Imagine, a pound of best steak for the dog!

The first office of the newspaper was set up at Clever Dick's house, when it was suggested that a professional editor was needed for the paper. The position was advertised in the national press, resulting in many applications. One of them came from a man we can call Mr Sinister, a highly qualified journalist and, it transpired at the three-hour interview with Clever Dick and the party representative, just right for the job. The appointment was duly confirmed by the party. Deadlines were set. Things were beginning to hum. A suite of offices was rented, more staff engaged. Mr Sinister noticed that Clever Dick liked to operate economically, he preferred crummy offices to smart ones, he thought that one man could do the work of three. And he did not want any truck with unions. The enterprise was shot through with cross-currents. Mr Sinister made a confidential phone call to the assistant secretary of the party, who confirmed that the party did endorse the principles of the union movement. All the same, he urged, Mr Sinister should go along with Clever Dick, who obviously knew what he was doing. These were early days and nothing to jeopardize the new paper should be entertained. Peace at any price. But as he continued to take on more and more staff, Mr Sinister was worried, because he had learned something about Clever Dick's background which seemed to have escaped the notice of the party. It started while he was still working in the improvised office at Clever Dick's house, and he happened to catch sight of a building society letter which threatened to foreclose on the mortgage for the house unless arrears of £500 were paid. This certainly did not tie in with the millionaire legend. Another factor was Clever Dick's casual mention one day that he owned a printing plant a few miles away. Mr Sinister checked up on this, too, and it turned out to be no more than a tin shed in which two young girls laboured over ancient machines, turning out letterheads and visiting cards, aided in the afternoons by Clever Dick himself. When Clever Dick threw a cocktail party to launch the new paper, it transpired that all the drink was on a sale or return basis. Again, it did not fit in with the millionaire image.

Clever Dick was not slow to utilize party resources and they, in turn, wanted to promote the new paper. Television appearances, radio and press interviews, they all came his way, and he became a well-known figure in a matter of weeks, his hallmark being an ability to speak his mind on practically any subject at the drop of a hat. The 'man of the people' image attracted many people. He was blessed with human understanding and wealth, and he often mentioned God, too, so it just showed what a good chap he was. There were hints that he might be adopted as a parliamentary candidate by the party. There was something as flamboyantly likeable and believable as the image presented by Horatio Bottomley, who conned millions out of the public during World War One. If some people derided his grassroots politics, it was only sour grapes. Not everybody loves a man who is successful.

The paper got off to a brilliant start, printed by a real printing company some miles away until, as Clever Dick kept pointing out, they got the plans passed for their own office block and printing works. He even produced the architect's plans for the premises. Mr Sinister, who examined the plans, refrained from saying that they seemed to relate to some other project. He was, in any case, far too busy trying to get the paper out on time. By this time he had recruited a number of writers from the party ranks, but he still had to write several thousand words a week to fill those great areas of white space. It was hard work. The second issue maintained the high standard. Subscription forms began to come in with money pinned to them. Mr Sinister spent part of his time trying to interest advertisers in buying space. Agreements with newsagents were made. It was gathering momentum. However, Mr Sinister had a folder full of overdue bills which Clever Dick refused to attend to, and representatives of the firms started calling, asking for their money. Mr Sinister gave Clever Dick's private address, hoping that the bills would be paid. Clever Dick was now dodging people. In the end it became too much, and Mr Sinister phoned the deputy secretary of the party, who arrived later the same day to investigate. It was obvious that all was far from well. In the next few days the secretary, treasurer and other officials of the party tried to see Clever Dick, who made excuses and avoided everybody.

Sensing trouble, Mr and Mrs Clever Dick and their accountant suddenly decided to issue the long overdue debenture bonds. It was a formality which they had overlooked. Once the documents were posted, they were covered.

Mr Sinister's last two salary cheques had bounced and so had those given to other members of the staff. By this time rumour and conjecture occupied more time than the job of getting the paper out. The party had at last managed to corner Clever Dick, who put on an act of being disturbed by their lack of trust. He instructed Mr Sinister to convert the newspaper into something else. It was re-titled, re-designed overnight. Clever Dick smugly explained that he had always wanted to own a newspaper.

One night, after everybody else had gone home, Mr Sinister waited in the darkened office, smoking and waiting. Several cigarettes later the door quietly opened and there stood Clever Dick. He stopped short. 'Ah—everybody gone, then?'

Producing the rubber cheques, Mr Sinister laid them on the desk. 'Tomorrow these will be met,' he said evenly.

Clever Dick hardly looked at them. 'A slight mistake, old chap. We're closing one account and opening another. I accidentally made these out on the closed account. It's all right, don't worry."

The party was now anxious for a reckoning. An extraordinary meeting was called for the debenture holders, and Clever Dick was invited to attend. He put on his best suit and took Mr Sinister and Mrs Clever Dick along to help him to face the music. But the music turned out to be rampant discord, for there was only one question to answer: 'Where's our money?'

'Your money is quite safe,' Clever Dick retorted.

'It's not being used for the purpose we decided.'

Clever Dick took a deep breath. 'We—that is, my company—are producing a newspaper for your party.'

'Is that so? You've changed it, you've pinched it.'

'I'm doing my best for you under the circumstances.'

There was a rumble from the hall. 'Then you'd better stop doing it.' Before Clever Dick could answer, a unanimous vote of no confidence had been passed and the meeting came to an end.

Less than one hour later Clever Dick was assuring Mr Sinister that they would carry on publishing the newly titled paper, and, as far as working capital was concerned, money would be found. He sounded so convincing that Mr Sinister decided to carry on for the time being and see what happened. Within twenty-four hours something did happen. Clever Dick phoned and told him to fire all the staff, but he should stay where he was and they would talk later.

On the other side of the fence the party secretary was in daily touch with the House of Commons. The MP felt impotent, especially after a meeting with the party solicitors, who told him that it was going to be very difficult to recover the £12,500 from Clever Dick. The eminent lawyer put the papers back in the file and looked at the MP, who was also a personal friend. 'You see,' he began as gently as possible, 'the debenture was raised within the party for the purpose of publishing a weekly newspaper and, as far as I can see, this gentleman has done just that.'

'Yes-yes-yes. But we know he transferred £2,500 to his other company—'

'Improper, I agree, but these things happen in business. If he puts it back into the debenture account . . . by the way, what name is this debenture account in?'

The sickening truth about the handing over of the £12,500 was admitted. It was also admitted that the money now rested securely in the account of the investment company to which only Clever Dick had access. The lawyer looked sad. 'That's about it, then. With a little more thought you could have avoided this mess.'

'But the money, the party—' The MP was practically inarticulate. 'We've got to get it back, every single penny of it. If the truth leaks out—'

'You'll have a devil of a job. Under the terms of the agreement, this fellow, or his company, promises to pay a certain rate of interest on the various sums loaned until the principal is repaid. If he pays the interest regularly on the appointed dates, there is simply no comeback. When does the principal fall due?'

'Some in five years, some in ten years,' groaned the MP. 'Are you trying to tell me that he's going to have the use of £12,500 at a nominal rate of interest for five to ten years? It's fantastic!'

As he was preparing to leave, the MP made one last appeal. 'I think I should have a second opinion on this, just to make sure.'

'Yes, it might be a good idea.' The lawyer mentioned a famous barrister. 'I'll send the papers over to him in the morning. By the way, did you subscribe to the debenture?'

The MP hesitated. 'As a matter of fact, no, I didn't.'

At the end of eighteen months and innumerable meetings with solicitors and barristers the party suddenly discovered that they had spent more than £2,000 on legal fees, but the £12,500 was still in the custody of Clever Dick, although they had by a strategem managed to freeze what was left. Exactly what that sum amounted to, nobody could discover. It could be £5, it could be £100, but it is almost certain that Clever Dick milked it before all the trouble started.

It was not for the first time that a political party had been well and truly done and it will probably not be the last, for political organizations are among the most gullible of all organizations.

Of course, a very strong stomach is required to play this game, and you might think that £12,500 is little enough for all those angry solicitors' letters, the savage meetings with the victims, and it is almost impossible even now to decide whether Clever Dick was a deliberate conman or whether he fell into it by sheer accident. It was perhaps a mixture of both.

Jacob, on the other hand, was honest about his operations. He could afford to be, because he was at the centre of more than twenty companies. He is getting on now, and has seen sixty. But after thirty years of financial manipulation he sees fraud as a normal way of life, calling for brains and intellect. If questioned he says: 'I am a business man, simply a business man.'

We met by prior appointment at a London hotel where he occupied a small suite on the top floor, full of new books which he ordered as a matter of course and which, once scanned, were given away to floor waiters and chambermaids. He sat, rather magnificently, in a gilt chair at the open window, the curtains flicking in the evening breeze. His 17-stone frame was wrapped in a Paisley dressing-gown, a white silk shirt and casual slacks with moccasins dangling from his bare feet. His face was dark and flat, and he smiled all the time until I reached him and shook his hand.

His son, Peter, took me on one side. 'Poppa is tired. Don't bother him too long.' He was a Cambridge graduate (Economics), polished and quite different from his father. I had known Jacob long before Peter was born.

'I have to go out, so you can talk,' he said. 'See you later.' Before departing he phoned room service and arranged for relays of Turkish coffee and pastries to be brought in. Without coffee and cakes life became impossible for his father.

The door clicked shut and Jacob invited me to sit down. 'Well, so five years have gone since the last time, eh?' He patted his chest. 'How am I looking?'

'As usual,' I said.

'I have a little chest trouble now and then. Too much smoking.' He laughed. 'Peter says see a doctor, so I do that. Some specialist, that one. Stop smoking, he says, and then he sends me a bill for twenty guineas.'

There is about Jacob a suggestion of Max Miller and Issy Bonn, but it is all front, and behind the flashiness there is steel and determination and they are an accurate reflection of what life has meant to a man who is now one of the main pivots of organized fraud in Europe.

He agreed that I might put some questions to him, and he would decide whether or not to answer them. For old times' sake, he grunted, he would try and help me.

Q: What were the early days like?

A: Not so bad, not so dusty. Things were easy, no complications. Everything I had I could hold in my hand. Today there are too many people in the business. I am just a Mr Big, saying yes or no.

Q: But you're better off?

A: Sure-sure-sure! I am rich, but what is rich? In the war it was black market, the marché noir, you know, for food, tyres, anything, stuff you could see and handle, and customers paid cash. Now it is ideas, all ideas, and today we sell ideas, things you can't see. That's the difference.

Q: Can you tell me where you came from, Jacob?

A: That's a no-answer question, but maybe I am a little Polish, a little this and a little that. My uncle was from Cairo. Imagine, Cairo!

Q: But you had a family life, didn't you?

A: Sure-sure-sure! I went to school right here in London. It's still there. Then after school I started learning tailoring and cutting and sewing and pressing. Good-class stuff, very good, up to £25 a suit all those years ago. But what's a kid got to work for? Look at Peter, my boy, university and all that. He's well educated, better than I was.

Q: When did you go into business on your own account?

A: Forgotten. Does that matter so much?

Q: What happened then?

A: What happened? I was surprised. You know what I found out? I find out how easy it is to make money. That's the first lesson I learned. Everybody has one important first lesson, even you.

Q: That's true.

A: Mine is money, a sense of business. My place in Basle, that was bought out of business. See my car? A Mercedes, very nice. That is business again. All the time it is business.

Q: Is that the only thing that interests you?

A: Aw now, wake up, boy! You think I'm so ignorant? Just last night I was at a concert with Peter and his girl. You see his girl? A popsy, very nice, only so thin. She likes me, says I'm a good poppa. We all went to this concert, then I said how about supper? So we went to some nightclub. Me, I like anything like that. The concert, it was pretty good, too.

Q: I'd like to ask you one question. Have you ever come up against the Mafia?

A: You're crazy! The Nostra is in one league, I am in another league. They like property, casinos, drugs, show business. My trade's not like that. Don't you know anything at all, boy? But I did meet Lucky Luciano once. Nice fellow, very sharp, he was getting fat, so I told him so, and he laughed and I thought god, this man has a funny sort of laugh. Well, maybe not so funny. He was asking me about my business. I forgot what I told him, just nothing of interest. Only years later I heard he was in the Mafia. Very frightening. About that time I was selling real estate in the Mediterranean. I was out there to see it—a half a square mile of desert in Tunisia, miles from any fresh water. That was before the real estate boom, but I did all right. Promoted it in London, sold it out in a few weeks. Made a lot of money.

Q: When you've made a killing like that and you've got a lot out of it, how do you feel?

A: Feel? I feel great. Anyway, I used to. Start with nothing, then find you've got £50,000 in the bank. How would you feel?

Q: But what about investigations? Surely you worry about the police?

A: Police? Listen, these things take a long time to get investigated. They are simple inside but from the outside they look complicated, and by the time the police move, that's the end of it. You're away, you're gone, you use another name, leave the country. What do the police find? Nothing but an empty office, that's all. Maybe no office even.

Q: Can I ask you a personal question? Don't you ever feel bad about it?

A: No. There's a little secret to it. Take what they can afford, sell them a cut-price dream. A fellow wants to go and live in his own villa where the sun shines. Okay, so sell him the land, sell it legitimately, give him a deed of ownership, give him his damn dream. He's happy and he goes on being happy, and maybe some day he goes out there and finds it's a swamp or a desert or something like that, there's no road in and no road out, but if he's tough he'll go right ahead and build his lousy villa and a road. Do I have to give him these things wrapped up with a ribbon round them? I sell him the dream, that's all I sell, and the dream is always different. Tell you one thing I found out; if you're German, French, English, any nationality, you always got the same dream. I dream about their dreams, that's what's so different about me. Just recently—well, some of my associates could tell you more—but we are hot on the franchise industry. There's legitimate franchise, like launderettes. You pay so much, you get their know-how, they fix you up with machines, shop decoration, that stuff. So, anyway, the profits are always good, or they seem to be, maybe as much as fifty per cent on the investment, and there never was a franchise scheme that didn't give you the idea that no work is involved. This is a magnet for the guy with the dreams. You see, we are still selling dreams! For his little investment of £3,500 or £5,000 he's going to get back £300 or so every week with very little work. That's a gold-plated plum! What's a politician except a seller of dreams? He gives a lower value. So just look at an election and this windbag goes round like a paid rainmaker in a desert, and he says okay give me the money, you get the rain and your crops grow again, and the politician says put me in and boy, life will be honey, you will never regret it. Is that fair? He doesn't even give them a parcel of lousy land they can maybe trade.

Q: Has your business changed?

A: No change. It's still the dreams business, that's basic. There's more dream to it now, that's all. We just started a new one on a small scale, it's a honey, but so old it was started in the Ark. I got a young German in association with me. Escaped from East Berlin some years back. Peter was over there, brought him back. We fixed him up. I thought this guy has a lot of brains but you would never have thought it. This Ambrose—it's the name he uses now—he's all squashed by the Commies. So I said to Peter we should give him time, he'll be an investment. He's so clever, knows the meaning of survival. We sent him to a Berlitz so he'd have better English and in no time at all you'd say this guy is English, you'd swear it. For a long time he doesn't know my business, not until we take him over to Switzerland, and then he meets my associates and somebody says to him, your friend, Jacob, is a smart one. He gives him the full lecture on me. So this is it! Ambrose admires me. Peter says Ambrose wants to repay me for all my trouble, and so on, but I said no, just tell him he's okay if he wants to go. He's a nice fellow, this Ambrose, nearly a second son to me, but there's no jealousy from Peter. It's great. Anyway, Ambrose works in our office at Basle, everything's fine and just a few weeks ago he produced a new idea based on an old one, and it's yielding a good dividend right now, up to £1,000 a week. How about that?

This was the scheme.

The first move was to secure the national rights to a piece of desirable equipment, perhaps a tape recorder, camera or midget television receiver. It had to have one or more special features, although this was not completely essential. The happy hunting ground for anything like this is Japan, where manufacturers are not unwilling to make distributorship agreements with visiting European business men. All that is needed is the purchase of specimen models or even one single model plus as much technical sales literature as can be supplied by the manufacturer. It is important to realize that the commodity itself is unimportant. One operator recently said: 'You could work this one with fur-lined chamberpots.'

As soon as the rights were acquired Jacob's assistants met in London and, under the direction of Ambrose, elaborated a basic plan. In this instance the focal point was a tape recorder, said to be the very last word in portables and bound to be attractive to the suckers. As a machine it did not measure up to portable recorders made in Europe and sold at a lower price, although it did look better with its chrome flashing and imitation leather facing in best vinyl.

A company was formed and registered, using proxy names. The names of Ambrose, Jacob and the 'think men' did not appear on literature or letterheads. The names were pinched out of the telephone directory, and lesser members of the company posed as these mythical individuals when a bona fide solicitor was retained, ostensibly to look after company affairs but purely for the sake of his name. The first national advertising was placed and published. In Britain the Newspaper Proprietors' Association and the professional institution of the advertising profession recently asserted the right to vet advertisers. A blue form is sent to new advertisers which must be completed before any advertisements can be published. On top of this, recent legislation prevents advertisers from making claims and statements which cannot be substantiated. While this has driven many shady companies right out of business, it has served to put the clever ones on their guard and increased their ingenuity.

The brochure material for the venture was written by a professional copywriter who worked as a rule for an international advertising agency but had for several years received a useful retainer from Jacob. It was a 'come on' advertisement which appeared in the Business Offers section of many newspapers. A minimum investment of between £350 and £500 was required and 'only men of integrity need apply'. The cautiously worded brochure was despatched to enquirers, singing the praises of the portable recorder. But even larger was a special offer to a 'select few' distributors to buy in and make a potential £1,000 or more a week. In no time appointments were being made and the interested parties were being interviewed. The mature-looking men who conducted the discussions had been through this and similar exercises for Jacob many times before, and they were experts. For a suitable fee they could sell anything to anybody. The applicants were obviously impressed by the offices of the organization. The desks alone looked worth a fortune, the carpets were unusually thick, the drapes at the windows were deep red velvet. And the refreshments! When each applicant represents a potential £350 to £500 one should, of course, be as lavish as possible with liquid refreshments. Care was taken to establish a system of graded interviews so that the would-be investor would feel that he was getting somewhere. In the foyer, near the shapely receptionist, stood the focus of it all, the portable recorder in a glass case, a spotlight on it. A demonstration was promised.

Who falls for this kind of thing? Many different kinds of people, from ex-Army officers with no hope of getting a job but with a certain amount of capital and a yearning to be masters of their own destiny; retired men with a hankering for business; those in search of a second string to augment their wages—in fact, all kinds of people, all of whom share the common feature of having money to invest.

It was made clear to applicants that a basic £350 distributorship was available, but for £500 a real piece of business could be bought and this would yield an entitlement to organize his own business, selling distributorships. In fact, the real aim was to sell distributorships rather than recorders. This seemed to surprise many applicants, but they agreed that selling distributorships was better than selling recorders. The bigger the promised rewards, the more greedy the suckers become. It is the principle of the now outlawed chain letter brought up to date.

Jacob resumed:

'Ambrose was so busy; one day it was Birmingham, next day Carlisle, next day Edinburgh, just keeping up with all those newspaper ads. Everything was scheduled to a timetable. And at the end of three months—why, that boy came back with a lot of money and the look on his face, it reminded me of my young days after a good killing. Ambrose, a boy with a magic touch. He came with a note of everything, showed me the figures in his books. And he wanted me to have a half as soon as he closed down. He was going over to Paris for a year or so. Next week Peter is going to see him. Maybe I'll go along, too.'

The essence of the Ambrose swindle does not differ very much from other large-scale frauds. It is simply a studied exploitation of avarice and greed, it involves the taking of money and the final letdown. While it is remarkable that so much time goes by before anybody starts making enquiries, it should be borne in mind that operators like Ambrose and his associates cleverly delay the time when suspicions are aroused by saying that certain documents would be forwarded and supplies were being flown in from Hong Kong. When such a fraud covers the entire country, the first indication is a few CID reports, a few letters to newspapers which published the advertisements in the first place. More time is lost while copies of the reports reach the Metropolitan CID if the 'head office' of the firm was in the City. By the time the hue and cry is raised, the Ambrose figure is far away at his villa in the sun.

One of the greatest problems when fraud of this kind is being practised on such a large scale is where to keep the money. Jacob, for instance, has vast deposits in more than eighteen countries, he has huge sums in investment trusts in Britain and America. But everywhere he placed money, it made more money, and for ten years his accountant was hard pressed to devise new methods of utilizing the increasing mountain of currency. Not unnaturally, a surplus found its way into a numbered bank account in Switzerland. This somewhat conventional arrangement did not suit Jacob, because the interests were low. He bought one or two London properties, grew dissatisfied, sold them at a profit and was back where he started. At a time when specialist unit trusts were coming into fashion, he launched one of his own to attract investment in electronics, putting £50,000 into it. Other trusts were started in several countries, dealing with investments in property, pharmaceuticals, agricultural chemicals and fertilizers. But the bigger it grew, the less Jacob was interested, and he took only £12,000 out of it as a director.

He was still smiling slightly as he watched me pouring out the last of the coffee. 'So . . . there it is. Plenty of money, plenty of time, no fun, eh?' His eyes went to the evening traffic and he said quietly: 'No fun at all any more.'

Mentally reviewing my depleted bank account, I agreed that when one is preoccupied with wealth, life can be tedious. Many millionaires were miserable people, I said, and he grunted, reaching for a scarf which he wrapped round his thick neck. Wealth, he was sure, could be useful up to a certain point, and it was obvious that after you acquired everything you needed and wanted, there was nothing more to be done. A house in any area of the world, a car when you wanted one, a few friends, a good son. . . .

Practically on cue, Peter arrived, full of talk about the play he had seen, a girl he had met, a thought he had just had. Jacob poured him a drink, and I left father and son with a promise that we would meet again soon.

Between the wars some ugly warts sprouted on the immaculate body of the City. They were called 'bucketshops'. They traded on greed at a time when large sums of money were hanging about, waiting to be picked up. It was at that time extremely simple to prepare and issue prospectuses devoted to mines in distant countries, diamond finds in Australia, oil in unlikely places. Not that the prospectuses lied. In many cases they did contain some seeds of truth. There is, for instance, gold in Nebraska and silver in Alaska. There is even gold in Wales in very minute quantities. Would-be investors lost not only their shirts but also their boots, and many a man was utterly ruined. All that happened in the 'thirties. The bucketshop operators drifted away, but one remained, and we can call him White-Black, which is not his real name.

White-Black calls himself an outside broker. While other brokers take the greatest care to avoid any hint of share-pushing, because it runs contrary to professional ethics, White-Black has for many years cheerfully pushed shares either on his own behalf or for a variety of shady characters. To understand how it is possible to function as an outside broker, it is first of all necessary to understand the structure of the Stock Exchange itself. There are two types of members, jobbers and brokers. The broker deals direct with the public, buying and selling all classes of securities, whereas the jobber specializes in a particular class of security and deals only with brokers and other jobbers. He makes his living from the difference between the prices at which he buys and sells, but the broker receives a commission from his client at a rate laid down in the rules of the Stock Exchange. You can obtain Stock Exchange membership by being nominated by a retired member, and this can cost money. A proposer and a seconder are needed. On entrance a fee of one thousand guineas must be paid, and there is a 250-guinea annual subscription. The Council of the Stock Exchange is necessarily sticky about admitting new men. It is like applying for a high-powered position, because full details of all previous work and positions must be submitted for examination by the Council. A three-quarter vote is needed for first-year membership, but this is by no means the end of it, because members are re-elected annually. The basic requirement is that the candidate must have worked for at least three years for a jobbing or broking firm, whether as an office boy or an envelope licker would appear to be by the way, and it is essential that a minimum three months' training on the floor of the House has been completed.

To be quite fair to White-Black, he did at one time set his heart on gaining membership of the Stock Exchange. He was fifteen and worked for three years in the office of a jobber, but, after a somewhat unpleasant matter involving five shillings which was missing from the stamp box, he felt that he had been branded, and in some mysterious way the entire Stock Exchange fraternity had a down on him, despite the fact that he scrimped and saved to send a 5*s* postal order to his old firm, emphasizing in a covering letter that it had been a purely temporary loan. They never even acknowledged it, but he later heard that the senior partner kept it in his desk drawer and it was used to lend point to the standard lecture to newcomers about the advantages of honesty.

White-Black ordered more drinks and lit a small cigar. We had met at Mooneys in the Strand—the Irish pub—because he loved the place. At that time there was a bank strike or a lockout of some kind going on in Ireland, and Mooneys was packed with noisy, red-faced young bankers who had come to London to obtain temporary jobs or simply to drink, because this was the only pub willing to give credit. We were served by the deputy manager of a Dublin bank.

'What a nice idea, being served by a banker.' White-Black scratched his bushy sideboards and adjusted his half-moon spectacles. 'Well, good health, my friend, your very good health. A good drop of stuff this, isn't it? Well, now, as I was pointing out to you, I started in business with a millstone round my neck, and very unjust it was. I mean, all for a measly five bob. But they were much stricter in those days and five bob was worth a lot more, and so I suppose one can appreciate their point of view. Of course, it was half my weekly wage, too. That's what they paid me, ten bob a week. At eighteen! D'you know, up to that point I was so career conscious, it just wasn't true! All those bowlers and pinstripes, I could just see myself like them. But then, after I got chucked out, things were far from chirpy. My father was outraged. They wrote and told him about the five bob. God, what a day that was. He actually beat me, and my mother, my dear old mother, she was in tears. I seriously thought about running away to sea or becoming a tramp, and all for that five bob. Anyway, the old man told me to go and get a job, any job, and I scrounged round until I found a position as an office boy with a firm of outside brokers.'

Outside brokers are licensed by the Department of Trade. They are the people who act as middlemen in handling shares. Banks, for instance, are licensed outside brokers, and so are insurance companies, pension funds, trustee savings banks and others, including many of the firms which are set up to advise customers. The reason for the licensing was the Prevention of Fraud (Investments) Act, and it was introduced to halt the activities of the conmen and their bucketshops in the heyday of City fraud. The Association of Stock and Share Dealers keeps a firm eye on the ethical side of outside broking and rigidly suppresses any attempts at share pushing. The outside broker is, however, in a particularly advantageous position, because his clients will generally regard him as the man with the inside information, and a tip from him will seem to be worth having. Most of them issue information sheets from week to week, but they have to be composed with the utmost care, otherwise the heavy boys from the Fraud Squad will start taking an interest.

It was this side of the business which White-Black now entered. 'My boss was a decent type, very solid, always ready to help. Came up the hard way, y'know, so he probably knew my problems. I really felt terribly guilty about the past until he gave me a good talking to and brought me to my senses.'

This was a small firm, just White-Black, two partners and a typist, and they all laboured in offices painted green and brown in one of the City alleyways. White-Black tidied up, opened the mail, taught himself how to use the spare typewriter and even managed to balance the petty cash. It was some weeks before he understood the nature of the business, and then he mustered up enough courage to ask his boss to recommend a textbook. This provoked some good hearty laughter, and both partners could hardly restrain their good-humoured mirth. Everything that needed to be known could be written on one side of a postcard! Within twenty minutes the young aspirant learned that the firm specialized in buying cheap stock from several stockbrokers. They would buy practically any stock as long as it was cheap. The actual industries to which the stock referred had no bearing on the deal. It could be a small oil company or a firm launching synthetic gemstones, the conversion of pulp or scrap metal, anything. Having secured the stock, they recommended it to their own clients at a slightly higher price, often in minimum parcels or lots. It was as simple as that and the profits could be considerable. It appeared that a number of jobbers with stock to sell were in the habit of first offering it to the outside brokers and, by a curious and entirely legal manipulation, the same stock could then be sold to the public. The jobber cannot sell direct to the public, but the outside broker is not 'the public' and this detour is still common. The real profit, however, comes from tipping off private clients and unloading as much stock as possible at a price which is below the Stock Exchange quotation which was forthcoming within a few days of the stock going on the market.

'It's so damn simple, y'know. The mystery of the City is a

load of guff, take it from me.' White-Black drummed the point home. 'It wasn't long before I was assisting my boss and one day I had three phone calls to make for him, confirming some buying and selling, and he just sat there, watching and listening, and after I told him they'd confirmed, he said, "Good. You've just made more than £3,000 for me." That was the profit. I couldn't believe it. Three thousand quid in less than ten minutes, and I was being paid less than a pound a week. He must have seen the way I looked, because he whipped out a fiver. "That's your bonus," he said. A fiver on three thousand. I ask you!'

But White-Black did not immediately plunge into a life of fraud and trickery out of sheer resentment over the £3,000 deal. On the contrary, he was only too happy to take the reward and say thank you. From that time onwards, though, he did pay much more attention to the firm's affairs with the result that he was promoted to keeping the books. Sums like £2,000 to £8,000 a month were common, even when the market was in a depressed state. One advantage of the outside broker was that he could advertise for clients, whereas the stockbroker was prohibited from doing so. Thus, when business was slow, national advertising was put in hand and it was noticeable that trade picked up at once. Brochures were sent out by the hundred and it fell to White-Black to service these enquiries. If only one per cent of these became clients, the profits were still considerable, so advertising and brochure printing costs were always well covered.

And then the war broke out. From 1939 until 1945 White-Black was otherwise engaged. He became an army major, used to the good life, and when demobilization time arrived he felt distinctly chilly. Both parents were dead, killed in an air raid, and the government, still in turmoil, had not yet set up a commission to deal with claims for compensation. His only asset was his gratuity. Instead of drinking it away, he started a tipster sheet, produced on an old duplicator, and, to his surprise, found several hundred clients at £1 a year. Within a few months he started a bulletin about the growing flood of government surplus goods at a time when dealers were setting up overnight. All the information was published in the Press, and his function was to bring it together to save subscribers the trouble of hunting through the papers. Together, the tipster and government surplus news sheets grossed more than £1,000 a year, which was a fair sum in the 1945–50 period. The prospects began to look good on the Stock Market, but he ignored the possibilities because he had the chance of buying for a very low figure a number of German patents which had been acquired by the British government and sold outright as a contribution to the retribution fund. Thousands of these patents were freely available, but industry, struggling to get on its feet in the postwar period, paid little attention to the fact. Being the man he was, however, White-Black reproduced them and sold hundreds of copies by mail order. He now claims that he made more than £2,500 out of the deal.

But now for the real killing.

The firm which he set up was surrounded by the myths he invented. From the outside it seemed that it contained the resources of dozens of investment counsellors plus an underground intelligence system which was on a par with MI5. White-Black himself composed the promotion brochure. The advertisements in financial journals and newspapers epitomized quiet confidence, secrecy and discretion. Fifty bulletins a year were offered for ten guineas, plus special supplements. A glorified tipster sheet such as this stands or falls on its results and the success which subscribers enjoy with their stocks and shares. This presented no difficulties as far as White-Black was concerned, for he based his forecasts on those in the newspapers. On top of this he provided an advisory service to subscribers, the charge being 15*s* per answer. To get the information he himself subscribed to another service, which charged only 10*s* per answer.

'People,' he observed, 'are bloody naïve when it comes to their investments. Widows with engineering shares, inherited shares in building societies. Everything predictable. I used to keep a copy of every opinion, and in time I'd really got enough to deal with any enquiry you could name. It really was sodding dull and the money kept coming in, so I employed a couple of middle-aged women to cut the stencils and roll them off and post the bulletin to all those fearful subscribers.'

'And it was very dull?' I suggested.

'Understatement of the year, but looking back it seemed to suit me, because it gave me a lot of spare time. I used to go to the races or pop in the pictures three or four times a week. Always was fond of a good film. Then suddenly I got damned well fed up with it all. I needed something new. I even thought of taking a job, except I'd got absolutely nothing to offer. I mean, I wouldn't have offered me a job, if you see what I mean.

I did apply here and there, and I went to one firm and got an interview with the personnel chap. It was for some kind of admin. thing. They'd advertised it, so there I was, sitting on the edge of my chair like a little boy after his first job. The personnel chap asked me a lot of silly questions. Background. Education. Experience. War. And so on and so forth. He kept rabbiting on at me, so I started on him. What was the job worth? He said I could start at about £1,300 if I got the job. Good God, I said, I make about £5,000 now. He simply didn't believe me, he thought I was trying it on, especially when I said that I could make £5,000 in my spare time, so God knows what I might do full-time. He said he'd let me know about the job, but he never did.'

It was partly out of boredom that White-Black started twirling other wheels of fortune, such as a scheme for developing land in Barbados. He was in touch with a land speculator in the West Indies who held title to a hundred acres of brush and swamp. The idea of selling it to British investors interested White-Black. He took another office, publicized the Barbados plum, drew up phony plans based on a rough sketch supplied by his partner, whom he had never met and knew nothing about beyond the fact that he had a wonderfully aristocratic name. Publicity was stimulated by advertising in papers. This happened some time before the present boom in land sales overseas. White-Black experimented with different methods of publicity, quickly discovering that one of the primary appeals of owning land in the West Indies was sheer snobbery. The deeds were designed by a commercial artist and embellished with wax seals and drawings of dolphins.

He sold about 800 parcels of land at about £350 a time, and promptly paid half of the £283,850 to his associate, transferring the funds through a series of banks. He made a quick sale of his Stock Market service and then went to live for a year or two in Rome. Now he was back, conscious of the fact that there had been a bit of a fuss about the West Indies deal, but it was all ancient history.

A man like White-Black has no weighty philosophy and there are many like him in the con-game. They have cultivated a front which is entirely convincing. A conman is always on duty, he has an amazing stamina and professes a great enthusiasm for life and endeavour, and it is generally impossible to reproach him about his way of life. That was how I felt about White-Black as we walked together through Trafalgar Square in the early evening. He kept looking at the pigeons. 'Busy little buggers, aren't they,' he said.

We parted.

White-Black was, of course, a small thinker and while he doubtless made a lot of money, he did not go to much trouble with his schemes, most of which were frankly opportunist and often created on the spur of the moment. In comparison with the big men in the business, he is a tiddler and probably all the safer for it, because when you are a colossus you are intensely vulnerable. Oddly enough, many of the figures in fraud on an international scale are physically big, like bears in lounge suits. Equally odd is the fact that many of them are Americans or Canadians.

Hank is not ostensibly a conman. He looks like something else, and he is good to everybody, including his mother, who travels the world with him, and this has made him into a devotee of the America momma-cult. Both of his ex-wives would be quick to admit that he has a tendency to think first of Momma and then of her nourishment and finally of his business. Momma often complains about the time he spends in the gym wherever they happen to be. Since the sauna bath was introduced, he has divided his time between this type of toning up and going for long runs in any nearby park. As a physical specimen he is superb, and he radiates fitness and a complete confidence in the future, but he never talks politics. And yes, girls, by all means, but as far away from Momma as possible.

This is not exactly about Hank and Momma, although much of what follows was devised by them over a period of years, and it is doubtful whether the structure of offshore banking would have reached its present dimensions but for their ingenuity. Purist students of human nature might find them somewhat sickening, but if regarded as biological specimens they are almost tolerable, even if Momma, large and colourful in her Pucci cocktail dresses does suggest a gross bird of paradise surmounted by a crown of blue-rinsed hair, and Hank resembles a giant pack of processed meat with a Jim Reeves voice. Presence is his hallmark. He has, he says, fronted so many operations that he puts a well-pressed suit before brains, but if you happen to have both, you could be a big leaguer. If you want motive, then it is necessary to appreciate the fact that early in life Momma and little Hank found themselves very much alone after Poppa lit out, grip in hand. Momma was glad to see him go. He drank. He got damn ugly after a jar. So goodbye, Poppa. She does not say too much about the intervening years, while Hank went through high school, but she did make a little money, which she invested, and lost everything in the crash of '29. So she started again, and this time did a little better because Hank was older and he helped her, apart from the time which he spent down at the public library, reading of all things the Wall Street Journal. From what little he knew about the crash, the one lesson he learned was 'never trust a firm you know nothing about'. It may have been the keystone of his later career. He was an office boy in a firm called Gelver in the hardware trade. Then a firm of bowling alley operators on the accounts side. After that he was in wholesale catering, again on the accounts side. The list lengthened, concluding with World War Two, and the curtain came down on the prospects for the future. Some years later he was adrift with a little money of his own, and he got caught up in the postwar building boom and managed to start his own company, building and selling low-cost chalet-type houses. The profits were small but regular, the routine irksome. In this hustling world of selling houses against time, borrowing money and repaying it, he was worried about his lack of future. Profits just had to be bigger, otherwise he could go on like this for years, and he would grow old, doing the same thing over and over again. Momma was naturally worried about what she now refers to as 'Hank's personality deterioration'. The boy was losing his morale, he was sinking, he needed a shot in the arm. She made it her business to examine her son's company from A to Z, and triumphantly produced a scheme. What she proposed was that Hank should start his own finance company. Or she could start one, because she had always thought it would be interesting to go into business. And phooey to the Monopolies Commission! The finance company operated in housing for a year or two, and then it spread out to small industry, ran into some bad times, recovered and then came under Federal scrutiny. At this point mother and son decided to leave for Europe.

Unlike many Americans, they lived in Liverpool instead of London. Then they went to Manchester and the Midlands. They loved England but it was not exactly Klondike. They packed up and went to the Continent, did Paris, Rome, Berlin and finally returned to London to become professional expatriates. Hank was more restless than ever. By this time he had cultivated a passable English accent and was a frequent partygoer, almost a

Hollywood figure and very attractive to the more mature woman. He had his fun without admitting too much to Momma who had now embarked on a round of museums and galleries, secretly worried by the fact that their money would not last forever but without any wish to return to the United States to face the Federal Commission, which had filed charges against both of them. She had prudently transferred practically all the company funds to Europe before the difficulties began. While they were able to live in high style at the moment, the capital was not making anything, it was just being eroded away. In the end she put it to Hank, hoping that he would have some ideas. Naturally, he did have ideas. During his period in real estate he had sold insurance on the side, sometimes as a corollary of mortgage agreements, sometimes as a safeguard for the casual worker who was subjected to periods of unemployment. Insurance, he thought, was a good risk on the law of averages alone.

He may have been right. In Britain insurance is governed by the rules laid down by Lloyds and these rules are the client's safeguard. There are two types of insurance, one of them designed to cover certain eventualities, such as injury in accidents. The second type is assurance, which means that the heirs of the insured person receive a sum of money on his death. The notion of Lloyds being willing to insure absolutely anything (such as the legs of a film star) is erroneous. There are many fringe areas which insurers will not touch. An author, for instance, would find it hard to insure against incapacity, because the insurers take the view that even if he is blind or loses a limb, he can still continue to pursue his calling as a writer.

Hank knew, just as others with a knowledge of insurance know, that risk is always over-valued. Comparatively few people become permanently incapacitated by accidents. Taken in relation to the total population, only a few lose their sight or a limb between certain ages and under certain conditions. The biggest profit in insurance comes, however, from lapsed life policies, because the cash-in value is always less than the total sum paid in. The companies say that the difference between the cash-in value and the actual value goes to cover the risk taken by the company, the administration costs and the 'general expenses'. In the meantime the insurance company has invested the premiums and the money continues to earn interest, and the sum paid to the client still leaves a residual sum which remains invested. At the last count the cost of running an insurance policy was proportionately high, Canada life being 23.61 per cent of premium income with the Prudential much lower at 13.44 per cent.

Hank began to look more closely into the whole field of insurance. Amongst other things he discovered that insurance companies are in the moneylending business in a big way and they own slightly more than the usual share of the national wealth. They lend money on the basis of a pledge of something which is always greater in value than the sum loaned.

During recent years the British government has grown more and more curious about the financial affairs of insurance companies and there have been some embarrassing revelations in which the accumulated wealth of certain concerns has been overwritten by a large question mark. In the view of some politicians, the insurance companies wield far too much power, and it has even been said that they will eventually be killed by their own wealth.

Hank came in at the tail end of the postwar boom in insurance. By the time he considered starting his own insurance company, a Socialist government was introducing legislation which suggested that any business man of any substance whatever would spend far too much of his time placating the Inland Revenue. Out of his sense of outrage Hank suddenly hit on the answer, offshore banking.

The offshore business boom has been with us for some years, and it came about because of the avarice of the governments of many countries which penalized business enterprise. Small countries such as Panama, the Channel Islands, the Bahamas, have been quick to offer business facilities, and lawyers in these areas have drummed up business in the heavily taxed areas with propositions to register or transfer business—on paper, at least—to these 'tax-free havens' with the object of handling their banking, insurance and book-keeping. What these areas would hope to gain out of it has always been a little hazy, but the obvious dividend is investment and a general growth of business. In its initial phases the offshore operation was entirely legitimate and it remains so. But for men like Hank. . . .

His first move was to establish his own bank in a Caribbean island with his mother and a seedy European nobleman as fellow directors. The nobleman was only too happy to allow Hank the use of his title for a down-payment of £1,000 plus £500 a year for a period of five years. In effect, by being an offshore bank, the company could write its own terms of reference, make its own regulations and still remain untouched by the British government. Hank was not the only one to set up a bank in the Caribbean without actually going there, but his bank was different because it went into business with only £2,000 capital. As soon as a letter of incorporation was received from a lawyer over there, he repeated the operation, this time in the Channel Isles. His bank was located in Guernsey. It existed only on paper but it was good enough. He then made himself president of the bank.

Within a few months dozens of advertisements were published in newspapers and magazines not only in Britain but throughout the Continent, offering car insurance and life assurance at about half the cost of the normal rates. The formalities were few and even elderly people were not asked to take the usual medical examination. Any low-cost proposition is bound to attract a certain number of clients. As one operator told me: 'Sell at £1 a time and make a million, sell at £500 a time and make a quarter of a million.' Hank's insurance offshoot was willing to insure any vehicle, sight unseen. During the first month or two several claims came in and were promptly settled, but when it was obvious that some clients were out to bleed the company, Hank hired his own assessors on a part-time basis. The growing wave of claims was kept under strict control, but advertising was stepped up. At this moment the takings amounted to more than £5,000 a week and the overheads were negligible. Hank relaxed slightly. From practically nothing to £5,000 a week was very satisfactory. Hank hired an investment counsellor to build a folio for himself and Momma. He also started similar companies in France and Germany. With only a negligible staff, he now shifted into a new gear and, in a massive promotion campaign, began to offer franchises, backed by the assets of his banks. Under this arrangement he sold pieces of the insurance companies at £1,000 a time, 50 per cent of the sales being paid into the parent company and 50 per cent being retained by the franchiser. Naturally, to cover the division of profits and make it worthwhile, policy premiums were upped and some impressive literature and a know-how manual were supplied with the offer of unlimited free advice. Franchisers who could hit a certain target in a certain time were given free Continental holidays. It is not known how many of these do-it-yourself insurance agents realized that virtually anybody could set up office and offer several dozen policies of a wide variety, acting as agents for well-known insurance companies, but Hank's set-up was irresistible. It looked special and the profits were high. As for selling, everything was provided. These policies sold themselves. The payment of £1,000 for the accumulated know-how of an international company which owned banks was neither too high nor too low. The prestige for the little man in the grey suburbs was magnetic. It was as Hank imagined it would be.

Some weeks after launching the franchise scheme, Hank discovered that more than forty clients were prepared to do business. The know-how manuals, which were carefully doctored versions of the manuals used by a different and entirely reputable American insurance company, were printed and passed out. Dossiers packed with useless advice arrived a few days later. Hank quickly passed the forty cheques, each one worth £1,000, through his bank accounts, most of the total £40,000 being used to pack the share folio, which had now grown. Most of the agents started up at once and were agreeably surprised to find that motor car policies at cut prices sold without any trouble at all. True, there was a sound of protest from Lloyds, but they were advised to disregard this. Under the terms of their agreement, they assiduously forwarded 50 per cent of receipts every three weeks. With the forty agents shovelling half their takings towards Hank's bank account, the cash flow was steady and continuous.

Hank now established a third bank at Nassau and this, in turn, was used to finance a number of land deals. By this time the network of companies, none of them with any statutory British or American registration, was practically beyond rapid investigation, so that by the time the Guernsey bank crashed overnight only a little ripple reached the police. Hank was nowhere to be found, nor was Momma. A few depositors who had been attracted by the promise of high interest rates actually went to Guernsey, only to find that the address was that of a solicitor who had handled the formalities of setting up the bank in the first place but was in no way implicated. The end of the bank was followed by the end of the now huge insurance network, but clients were readily taken over by the more solid concerns who had warned them against the dangers of cut-price insurance.

It seems unlikely that the offshore bankers will be able to continue using the Channel Isle of Guernsey as a base very much longer, because whereas virtually anybody could start a bank without too much difficulty, the Finance Committee has now decided that financiers wishing to use the words like 'bank' and 'banking' in their titles will have to satisfy them that they meet the approved definition. Even so, as Hank would say, there are still ways and means in Panama and the Bahamas.

Chapter Three

Today is a Gold Brick

So it is. Perhaps today sees the curtain going up on a fraud which may entice as much as £10,000 out of the pockets of the gullible within only a few hours or days. Or it may take a little longer. Behind this coup there may be years of planning. Or maybe it was hatched in a couple of days. It depends on what it is. There are old gold bricks and there are new ones but very few entirely new ones. Swindling the State is traditional in many countries, and the biggest case in recent years involved four Spanish gipsies, two Frenchmen and one woman who managed to get £2 million out of the French government by registering non-existent children and then claiming social security benefit. They had five cars, a trunk full of jewellery and a large bank account. Nine members of the consortium forged the papers which claimed the birth of more than 3,000 babies during a period of eight years, and one couple drew £440 a month in respect of 70 children, although no children existed.

During 1970 two men were charged at York with obtaining £42,000 from a wealthy woman said to be worth £100,000 by telephoning her in the middle of the night and saying that the caller was God. She was instructed to give away large sums of money to a national charity. His two chosen instruments would naturally take care of it for her.

A Jamaican who landed in Britain in 1954 with only 17*s* 6*d* in his pocket appeared in court in 1970 to plead guilty to four charges involving a total of £13,750, the result of a mortgage swindle perpetrated on the Greater London Council and the former London County Council.

During 1970 the Consumer's Association revealed a case of a surveyor who, by various means, was able to earn fees costed at £33 10*s* per man-hour spent on a site. In one experiment, when twelve surveyors were invited to estimate their charges for surveying the same Victorian house in London, their fees ranged from £21 to £95, the time taken being between $1\frac{1}{4}$ and 9 hours.

Elsewhere in Britain, when a house is on the market and a surveyor's report is required, several building societies may engage the same surveyor. He makes one report on the property for a fee, and then sends copies to subsequent enquirers, charging the same fee over and over again without ever going near the property.

Since 1955 new religious bodies have sprung up, some reputable and some dedicated to only one thing, making money. It is not generally realized that anybody can set up a church. No licence is required. The techniques vary. One much-used method is known as 'the tithe' whereby adherents are pressurized into giving 10 per cent and often more of their income to the 'church' for good works. The good works consist as a rule of depositing the money in the private bank accounts of the organizers. One self-styled reverend has made £2,000 a year for at least 25 years, making such a nuisance of himself that many nervous old ladies have been scared into giving him money.

In recent years the loan sharks have moved into the 'second mortgage' racket, taking advantage of successive government credit restrictions to boost their business. It is not uncommon for the victim to find that he owes as much as £630 or more for a £500 loan with the shark holding his mortgage. Many of these second-mortgage firms have mushroomed throughout Britain, taken the preliminary 'negotiation fee' of up to £100 and then vanished completely.

Immediately before this book went to press a new insurance firm enrolled more than 9,500 men who wanted to be self-employed in a scheme to sell security. In a lightning swoop they relieved all the applicants of a ten-guinea entrance fee and then vanished with a promise to be in touch within ten days. They never did. Ten guineas multiplied 9,500 times is a lot of money.

These are all recent cases, most of them occurring during 1970. Most of them suggest individual enterprise. It is when a national fraud is perpetrated, such as the one above, that the business begins to look like a business which is as co-ordinated as D-day. Indeed, this is precisely what it is, controlled by a handful of men. The concept of a group of individuals sitting down and planning in cold blood a huge fraud is not fiction, it is reality. It does occur several times every year either in Britain or within the Continental area. It is immensely profitable. Such operations are not necessarily single attempts, they are simply links in a chain.

All this was patiently spelled out to me by a man of about 50. His attitude was one of feigned indifference. It was only money, he said, so what the hell? He had been in and out of crime all his life and he had learned a lot about life and living while in prison. On the last occasion, when he was discharged, he tried to get a job but couldn't, and so he packed up and went to Paris, a city he had often wanted to see. He had a couple of thousand pounds of his own money and he thought that something might turn up. As a man he is not entirely unlikeable. By professional criminal standards he has a higher intellectual standard than many of his contemporaries. After several years of working for an organization in Paris, he has much more presence and self-assurance. It started when he picked up a regular girl friend in Paris She introduced him to a few of her acquaintances, none of whom seemed to work for a living. He was pleased by the way they accepted him. Every city in the world has people of this kind, but they should not be written off as moneyed layabouts. They are in their various ways quite industrious and they do work extremely hard.

The Paris conmen are well known. Stand in a gallery for a few minutes and look wealthy and self-possessed and you will probably be approached by a fellow who wants to sell a 'masterpiece'. Go to the couture shows and a beautiful girl will attach herself to you to offer pirated designs. Christian Dior once tried to turn detective and smash this trade but he was unsuccessful. If this sort of thing goes on more or less openly, then heaven knows what is happening behind those silver-grey louvred shutters in the business buildings from which nobody ever seems to emerge and which nobody ever enters.

It was behind such shutters that the Englishman was introduced to six people who thought that he might be interested in a job. The offices were innocuous but still prosperous-looking. The biggest place in the suite was the boardroom, tricked out in gold and scarlet, with a wide table on which papers were scattered. As he was ushered in, everybody stood to be introduced. One rather peculiar feature of this formal ceremony was that they all had the same name and yet they did not look like brothers. In fact, two were English, one was Spanish, another was German and three were French. Then the door opened and thre middle-aged women filed in. They were not introduced but took their places in silence. The men then explained that everybody in the room was a director of the business. Now, perhaps they could explain why they had invited him to attend the meeting. His girl friend had already mentioned his difficulties to them and they could perhaps help him. Although they went to great lengths to suggest that the firm was a very busy one, they did not mention the actual nature of it. When he asked them their line, one of them murmured that their business was making money. Before he had time to digest this, they said that they would advance him several thousand francs until he settled in and he would then be paid in the form of a handsome bonus per job.

He was still very much in the dark when he reported for duty some days later and went into conference with one of the men, who produced a file for him to read. It seemed to relate to a trades directory of some kind. Drafts of invoices and statements ready for printing, circular letters and lists of several thousand addresses were also enclosed. The letterheads concerned a firm with a London address. After going through it and feeling even more baffled, he laid it down on the desk and looked expectantly at his mentor.

'I will explain. This is extremely simple. There are 10,000 names on the list. They are firms in various trades, big firms and small firms. You know what a firm is like? It has management, it has an accounts department. In many English firms they are very old fashioned, it is still the same as in the days of Dickens. So, we send invoices to all these firms and they are for small sums, unimportant sums up to five pounds, but no more than five pounds. The invoices arrive, and on the invoice is something like "to entry in trade directory". Every firm appears in a trade directory of some kind. So the accountant sees the letterhead, he looks at the small sum, it all looks real. Some firms have one account for payments up to twenty pounds and other accounts for the big payments. In many the accountant has the power to sign the small cheques or maybe a junior director signs the cheque when it is passed by the accountant. So the invoice is paid. We receive two guineas, three pounds or more . . .'

The new recruit nodded brightly. 'I get it. Your firm publishes the trade directories.'

'We do not publish anything.'

'Well, you're agents for the publishers of the directories, is that it?'

'We are not agents. We are simply collectors of money. It is part of your job to go to London and post the letters. The replies will be forwarded from London to our office in Hamburg and then sent on here. This is necessary. We prefer long lines of communication. We use many addresses, you will find.'

'Do all these firms pay up?'

'Of course not. You will find that only a certain percentage will pay at once. The rest—forget them. There will be a number of queries. We ask the firms to forward the invoices and statements for investigation, and that is the end of it.'

'Why do we ask for them back?'

'They are evidence. Practically none of them take photo copies or make a proper record. They are glad to get rid of the invoice. So . . . that is your operation. You will be in charge of the operation. We will provide tickets to London and your hotel reservation is arranged. As soon as you have finished, you will return. In a few weeks the money will be arriving. You will also attend to that.'

The great fake directory scheme came to light during the winter following that summer, when most firms had staff depletion due to the holiday season. More than £8,000 was received within two weeks of despatching the faked invoices. In the third week a further £3,000 came in, and there was a rapid move to push the cheques through for bank clearance. Funds which accumulated in a British bank were filtered at speed to a Swiss bank, which offers the facility of numbered accounts.

I asked the man who had so neatly been ensnared how he felt about it once he received his large slice of the commission. Jubilant? Elated at the thought of such easy money? Over the moon?

'It kept me busy for a month or two, but after I'd got my cut there was a fantastic sense of anti-climax, like climbing a mountain then realizing you're up to the top and you've got to come down again. It was hard slogging while the money came in through Hamburg. They left me to it, but they'd got it buttoned up tight. Not a chance to fiddle a penny. They were very straight with me until it dawned on me that all they really wanted was a kind of fall guy just in case anything went wrong in England while I was there, running it.'

'You've been at it for several years now. What do you really think about it?'

'Well, it's not all the fake directory stunt. There are others, you know. You just don't go on pulling the same dodge all the time. We've done so well we only operate three or four months of the year, the rest of the time we spend planning, like any other business. It's the most normal thing in the world to us. We do a hell of a lot of research. We even hire consultants. We've got a man looking into business in Italy. We're interested in lotteries in Italy, not necessarily because we are putting one in there. It might be possible to try it on in some other country. We've moved into Denmark and Sweden. Research might go on for years, then we might drop it in the end. Sometimes I have to pinch myself and remind myself that we're not exactly legitimate. You get into a very queer frame of mind. The plan itself is more interesting than the actual execution. I mean, if you were doing several thousand people out of a few pounds each, you wouldn't lose much sleep over it. I can tell, you just wouldn't. You get to the point of not caring. You spend time convincing them that they ought to invest a fiver or a tenner and if they can afford it, they fork out. But if a chap can't afford it, he says so or he should say so. So why lose sleep? In any case, it's not as though we are pushing a chap up against a wall in a back alley and threatening to do him unless he forks out. Most of the time it's some investment scheme or other. They are all variations of the same plan . . .'

As we already know, it does take a considerable time before people discover that they have been rooked, especially if they have received an official-looking receipt for their money. If the racket concerns insurance, they do not expect to receive a copy of the policy for several weeks. The essence of such a project is not to appear over-generous. One would hardly, for instance, offer £25 a week for life on the basis of a £2 per year premium. On the other hand, the phony offer must contain something more than the sort of policy which can be obtained from any bona fide insurance company. In the last three years 'free' coverage of all dependents of any age, 'free' insurance of any type of pet from bears to budgerigars, a 'premium' bonus in the event of loss of limb, sight or mobility have all been offered. It is very much the technique of the 'loss leader' in the supermarket, when something of seeming value is virtually given away simply to get the customers inside the place, where they will buy the merchandise. There is, of course, nothing particularly dishonest about the loss leader technique, but the French organization has found it useful in conditioning the public to the idea of getting something for nothing. Nowadays the traditional come-on of the conman does not have to be quite as hard or as laboured as it used to be.

After being involved in so many of these get-rich-quick schemes the English front man has come to the not entirely novel conclusion that his associates were probably among the most gifted men in Europe. On the basis of the schemes which he described to me, there seemed to be something in his claim. I was rather impressed when he told me that he had seen one of the 'directors' studying Edward de Bono's book, *The Use of Lateral Thinking* (Jonathan Cape, 1967). It is a book which is said to take logic and reasoning out of the penny-farthing class of thinking. One cannot help wondering how the author, a former Rhodes Scholar to Christ Church, Oxford, and a Cambridge Ph.D., would feel on knowing that his theories were being put to such uses. It is a fact that the high-class conman must have more than a passing interest in the laws of probability and risk. If one can compute the chances of, say, a suspension bridge being blown more than .0001 out of true by a Force 7 wind, then the same technique can be applied to an operation which is designed to produce, say, £50,000 in a period of months, particularly if the variables of human psychology are substituted for the behaviour of physical materials. After all, a good copywriter can evaluate the effect of certain emotive 'trigger-words' which he uses when writing copy for advertisements and other promotion materials. This could well be the pattern of fraud and white-collar crime in the next decade. In the meantime, some hoary old confidence tricks are still being decked out in new clothing, and they achieve results which are not to be sniffed at. As a successful conman once told me: 'You know what a sucker is? It's a fish that will bite at a bare hook.' With which he slammed the door of his Bentley and invaded the London traffic, proud and brave and probably quite sure that he would never see the inside of a cell. On the basis of statistics and some research I am sure he would be right, because while the going is good the conman lives better than the rest of us. We work laboriously while he literally bursts with ambition and has far more confidence than we possess in situations which call for an iron-clad stomach. If a lot of us are Mitty-like heroes, many of us must secretly envy the ability of such people to accumulate super-super-tax incomes without as much as anxiously searching the job advertisements. A Fraud Squad officer said: 'Conmen aren't nits, they are the emperors of crime. Not that we see much of them . . .'

Some conmen like to stay in the background, but others love to hog the limelight, like George Augustus Jennings. You could love Jennings for his nerve and his personal vivacity. Few men fresh out of prison with a background of several periods 'inside' would have the neck to bluff themselves into a situation in which he was adopted as Parliamentary Candidate for North Paddington, London. He had only 3*s* 8*d* to his name at the time, but he did manage to obtain 6,444 votes with his personality and oratory, and even after he had been exposed as a conman it was widely felt that he would have made a first-class Member of Parliament. His backers were probably right, for politics is, as they say, the last refuge of rogues. Jennings planned his application at a psychological moment, when the Liberal Party was in travail and in need of new blood. With his invented Army background—commissioned, of course—and his impeccable manners, he made strong men pause in their tracks and women to curtsy. The trappings which he used were staggering, for he travelled by Rolls-Royce with a chauffeur. When he spoke about the state of the country he waved his monocle and was quick to point out firm lines of action which suggested that he had, in fact, devoted a great deal of thought to the Liberal Party and its problems. No sooner was he out of his adoption meeting than he appeared at a local bank where the manager was so impressed by the new Liberal candidate that he readily advanced him £21 10*s* for sundry current expenses. Jennings tossed a cheque for £1,500 on the desk and said that it could be used to open his account. He then called a meeting of a sub-committee of the area Liberal Party and talked £250 out of them for his current political expenses. For a few days nothing happened, and then the bank manager appeared, fluttering the £1,500 cheque, which had bounced. Jennings squinted at him through his monocle and suggested that he hang on to it for a few days, then it could be presented again. The sum was, he said, part of a legacy from his father-in-law, and those damned solicitor chaps obviously were not up to the task of administering the estate. Mollified, the bank manager bowed himself out.

By this time the Liberals were seriously disturbed by several tales which were circulating about the new candidate, who kept borrowing sums of money from all and sundry, and he was dropped overnight. Infuriated by what he considered to be petty bumbledom, he stood in the election as an Independent and then had a stand-up row with the returning officer, who refused to return his deposit. When the matter of the bouncing cheque came up yet again, Jennings was arrested and sent down for four years. As soon as he was set free, he invaded the by-election industry and, after a trick involving the Islington candidate, General Critchley, and £75 worth of cigars, he finally merged with the background and became one of the crowd, but only for a few months. The limelight was too much for him, and he became two bishops, one after the other. The first one was the Bishop of Coventry, the second the Bishop of the Falkland Islands, in which guise he descended on the then Lord Cowdray. His Lordship saw before him an entirely credible churchman, all gas and gaiters, who wanted to discuss starting a home for the destitute. Cowdray gave him a cheque for £50. The Bishop next called on Sir Louis Baron, the industrialist, who listened to a similar story, this time embellished with case histories. Thinking that he might perhaps help the project in a substantial way, Sir Louis asked the Bishop to write to him so that he could discuss the various possibilities with his directors. Having come this far, the Bishop sensed a very big sucker within biting range of his hook, and so he hastened to write the required letter on Carlton Hotel notepaper, inferring that a donation of about £2,500 would enable the work to proceed. Sir Louis fell for it and sent the cheque to the Rev. P. G. Jackson at a Maida Vale address. A day or two later another Carlton Hotel letter arrived, thanking him for his generosity. Once more something went wrong, and 'Bishop' Jennings was sent down for three years. No sooner was he out, having earned remission, than he was haunting the West End under a number of titled names, ordering luxury goods from the best stores and paying for them with rubber cheques. Everything he obtained he sold to ready buyers, the West End clubs amongst them. This self-defeating exercise finally carried him straight into the arms of the law and he went to prison for five years.

Nowadays we do not have many colourful Jennings figures. The modern tendency is to set up the corporate swindle. The people behind the swindle are not up to Jennings' flamboyancy. As often as not they are semi-qualified crooked accountants or men who have had a taste of industry and commerce and become fed up with routine work and poor rewards. And there is at least one woman. Female fiddlers are rare birds and, when they know their business, they can be quite intimidating. The one I have in mind was among the first in the wig boom, cosmetics by post, sexology and other rackets, most of them worked by mail. Her trail of bandwagons was long and impressive, and it had in its time produced enough money to pay for two houses, one car after another and holidays in the Bahamas. She had sundry bank accounts and investments. And she also had Claudia, her daughter. This thin, poetess-like wraith was a legacy from the far past, when her mother slipped up. It may have marked the beginning of the bitterness which flung Mother into a life of fraud, because she was left practically destitute. In the belief that she could earn an honest living, she took a job with a West End antique dealer. Her job was to float around the showroom, talking to buyers and answering the telephone. As a job it had no future, and her boss was interested only in profits. One day he sent her with a message to a sculptor's studio on the outskirts of London, and while she was there she noticed several dozen figures on a bench. They looked remarkably like some of the antiques in the showroom. Believing that she knew what was going on, she egged the sculptor to tell her more. He let the cat out of the bag about the trade in fake antique carvings. That night she returned to proposition him. If they worked together, she said, she would act as his agent and sell his work. They did very well at it for several months, and she was able to accumulate enough capital to consider her next step, which was selling shares in a non-existent mink farm in Scotland. In the early stages she did think of starting the farm, but the sight of several thousand pounds in her bank account got the better of her, and she did another name change and vanished only to reappear as a limited company devoted to co-operative pig farming in the Midlands. It was one of several concerns operating on the principle of 'own a pig and reap the profits', the appeal being to the yeoman instincts of the average Englander. Some of these firms were authentic in that they actually owned vast herds of bacon pigs, others were less than pie in the sky. Once more mother and Claudia moved rapidly, this time to the Lowestoft area, where they stayed long enough for Claudia to attempt her GCE, gaining Advanced levels in Economics, which is a most useful subject with many applications. Girton was in the air, but she was finally placed in a finishing school. Mother was constantly irritated by Claudia's total lack of personality, and she often likened her to a bottle of milk, white and bland and unattractive, while she herself was in the gin and whisky class. The idea that she dominated the child to the exclusion of all attempts at personality development never seemed to occur to her.

Mother's fault is that she is so full of nervous energy that she does not really see other people, and her social life is such that she does not seem to need love and affection. She has become so self-contained as to be unapproachable. This may spring from her early marriage to Claudia's father and the let-down, because she has not since then treated men with anything more than a superficial disdain. At forty-three she was the owner of more clothes than she could wear, two cars and a roof over her head, and she suddenly developed the habit of taking holidays on the spur of the moment 'to get away from it all'. She was in Ibiza when she met the actor.

He had once been a big name, now he was fading fast with a past full of divorces and one role after another. He was not so much a face as an institution. Mother took one look at his slim figure, the greying hair and the famous presence, and then made a beeline for his table, where he sat alone, and from the very beginning they got on very well. By the fourth day she had him in bed with her and after that just happened to interest him in a new business venture which could give him a thousand a year without him doing a single stroke of work. He was very vulnerable where money was concerned, because he had nothing apart from his small income and fees for one or two television plays every year. All she wanted, she said, was his name as sponsor of a new firm with which she was connected. In a haze of drink, food and mother's charms, he signed a draft agreement which she scribbled on a sheet of hotel notepaper, promising to get it done properly as soon as they were both back in London. As it happened, she left Ibiza before the actor and, within a few hours of arriving home, she had called in her tame promotion man and briefed him about a franchise plan. A new business name was registered at once, and the first advertisements emblazoned with the star's name were in the Sunday newspapers the following weekend. The firm, said to have offices in London, Paris and Hollywood, offered franchises to people who wanted to achieve independence for a down payment of only £250 with the prospect of huge profits. The £250 bought a kit of beauty aids and with it came a booklet, instructing the new business moguls how to promote sales on a door-to-door basis. Put in these terms, it does sound hollow and unconvincing, but the promotion brochure invested it with so much colour and glamour that during the first ten days eight cheques for £250 each arrived. It is a curious psychological fact that in many spurious promotions it is easier to worm a cheque for £250 out of the public than to sell something which is entirely legitimate for ten shillings. No sooner was the show on the road than two complications arose. The first was the appearance of the faded actor, who had seen the newspaper advertisement and objected hotly to the way his name was being used. Mother heard him out and then barked at him to sit down and shut up. She then shoved a cup of coffee in his hand while she hunted for her cheque book and scribbled one out for £1,000 cash. As she slipped it into an envelope, she gave him some sound advice. All he had to do was keep his mouth shut. If he behaved himself, she would take him out now and then. And she might even treat him to a holiday whenever he was in need of a rest.

Her second difficulty was in finding stock for her first eight clients, who had up to this time received nothing except receipts for their money, and, as time was going by, it was imperative that they receive something to keep them quiet. She hurried to the East End to see the wholesalers, her bag stuffed full of cash. The wholesale 'bunce' trade is legitimate except that the merchandise is generally sub-standard. It is sold in bargain stores and on fairgrounds in huge quantities, and some indication of the prices may be gained from towels at 8*d* each, picnic sets at 10*s*, children's dresses at 2*s* 6*d* each. A lot of the stuff comes from the sweatshops of Hong Kong, other lines are drawn from the stocks of bankrupt businesses sold for a song on the order of the Official Receiver. Many of these warehouses look like huge jumble sales, others are run on a cash-and-carry basis, but all are stuffed with stock. For £300 to £500 you can instantly fill a small shop. Whether you will sell the stuff as quickly as you bought it is another matter.

In her new role as a super-shopper mother quickly located a wholesaler with floor after floor of cheap cosmetics, including toilet water at 10*d a* bottle, lipstick at 15*s* a dozen, face powder almost given away. At a first glance the black and gilt packaging was tasteful and attractive, but a closer look betrayed its shoddiness. She struck a deal with the manager to pack eight large cases and use her own labels for despatch.

Advertising was stepped up until she was spending £1,000 a week on space in newspapers and magazines. It is a peculiarity of mail order that the conversion ratio of the response will always be a minimum of 1 per cent and if it rises to between 2 per cent and $2\frac{1}{2}$ per cent, you will be doing extremely well. Mother kept a close eye on her conversion ratio and she also upped the franchise investment figure to £300, finding that it worked even better than at the earlier £250. The promotion literature was re-written, and, unfortunately, she slipped in a sentence which claimed the firm manufactured its own cosmetics and had three main factories. But for this she might still be in business, but a trade journal of the cosmetics industry somehow got hold of a copy of the brochure and decided to investigate. Their report to the effect that Mother refused to give the whereabouts of her factories triggered off a national newspaper. A well-vetted article on Mother duly appeared, including an interview with the film star and analysis of the cosmetics kit supplied to franchise investors for £300. It turned out to be worth less than £12. The office was hurriedly closed down and Mother disappeared yet again with Claudia in tow. Her main supplier in Houndsditch was disappointed. 'A nice lady like that, a shame, a crying shame. She was okay, always the cash and a bottle of something every week. Is business enterprise such a crime these days? She was a proper lady, she always paid straight cash, not like some I could tell you.'

Chapter Four

The Modus Operandi

Any firm of any size would confirm that they have to employ a correspondence clerk to deal with complaints. It is a poorly paid job, done as a rule by an elderly man who knows something about human nature. Many of these complaints are, to put it bluntly, attempts at fiddles and they originate from small firms which are short of ready money or else play this game as a matter of course. If they keep at it long enough, they may get the account deferred or credited, or they may even receive a free replacement. It works the other way round, too. A friend of mine had a bookshop and he somehow became the target for a new and unscrupulous publisher of worthless textbooks and books for university students. At first he thought there must be some mistake, and so he wrote to the publisher, saying that he was returning three cartons of books and asking to be reimbursed with the carriage. In the next few days he was surprised to receive a bill for the books. He returned it at once with a covering note saying that the books had been returned. A week or two later more books arrived, this time in a more expensive price range and reaching a total of £165. He did the same thing again, but in due course received another invoice. Then monthly statements began to arrive. By this time his small stock room was jammed full of cases of books, which he had not even bothered to open. Then he happened to hear a radio programme about inertia selling, and it dawned on him that he was the victim of this technique. It appeared that other booksellers had been showered with cartons of books and, in the less well organized establishments, the bills had been paid without question. The storm was blowing up to gale force in bookselling circles when the publisher was fortunately taken over and that was the end of it.

Trade is one of the most fertile compost beds for the type of fraud which cannot quite be pinned down, although the victim knows very well that he is being done. As the lawyers never tire of pointing out, knowing and proving happen to be two very different things. This was what Wally traded on. I went to school with him, but we did not meet for years and then we bumped into each other at a London conference concerned with, of all things, industrial security. I knew it was Wally from his nose, broken in two places in school brawling, and his frizzy hair, which looked just the same. The only difference between the young Wally and the middle-aged Wally was the cigar. At school he used to smoke Woodbines. He was delighted to see me and kept addressing me as 'mate', because he obviously could not remember my name. When I asked him what he was doing at the conference, he winked theatrically: 'Learning myself a thing or three. Got myself invited with some other blokes in industry. What's wrong with that? I got my own firm. Electronics. Why don't you pop out and see us some time?' He produced an engraved trade card. I had never heard of his firm and said so. 'No wonder,' he chuckled. 'We do a lot of sub-contracting, mate. We don't make and sell, we make and sweat!' Delighted with his own wit, he repeated the invitation and trotted off to take his seat for the next lecture.

It was not much of a factory, just a collection of concrete buildings on some wasteland about thirty minutes from Marble Arch. There was no path or road, just a track across the gorse. Wally appeared in his shirt sleeves and showed me round. There was very little to see, simply battered trestle tables at which young boys and middle-aged women put together electronic components. Conditions were abysmal in the extreme with rough stone floors and gaps in the walls stuffed with oily rags and newspaper. Wally apologized for the makeshift canteen, and said that he had lost his last factory. A terrible fire. Somebody must have left a soldering iron on. All this was temporary until the insurance company coughed up. He stood to make quite a bit out of it, because the lot went up in an hour, insurance cards and all. Not a trace of anything, just a load of black ash, helped, he thought, by the carboys of acetone and other fluids in a back room.

Something in his voice made me watch him more closely. It was remarkable that he could treat what had obviously been a catastrophe so lightly. He admitted that he had lost several good contracts into the bargain. It was the kind of thing which would put a small firm out of business.

'You're kidding,' he said. 'You don't know business, mate. So we lost out on it. The firm was only my wife—you must meet Miriam—and me. She knows damn all about it, she's just a name on the notepaper. This business is me, win or bust. I worked like hell to keep going.' He glared at me, a slight film of sweat on his red face.

About a year later a file was passed to me for an opinion. It originated from a trade association. These trade associations are essentially 'clubs' formed by the individual trades for the purpose of exchanging information, marketing news and technical advances, and they also share research facilities in some instances. On the darker side, many trade associations do their own intelligence work to protect members, hence the file which was before me. It was literally bursting with papers of all shapes and sizes, and it was some time before I could discover that it related to Wally's firm. Had he seen it, I am sure he would have burst a blood vessel.

Wally was a sub-contractor, and he ordered his raw materials from many different sources. The list in the file detailed 150 firms with experience of his business methods. It appeared that he would send first to several firms for samples of, say, wire. In business a sample of wire can be a large quantity. For instance, a pound of aluminium wire of .75mm diameter is hundreds of yards long. Wally wanted copper wire, and at a time when he was not yet known as a shyster, several firms obliged, submitting a total of twenty reels of wire. The same method was applied to other materials, and he obviously did very well out of it. Hard on the heels of the samples came the technical representative to see Wally and try to get an order. Of course, a technical representative must have an understanding of his client's wants, and for a long time Wally was treated with great deference. He was taken out to lunch, provided with hospitality, and he said that his 'quality control' department was examining and testing the samples. In this way he managed to build up a substantial stock of materials, and the representatives gradually faded away with a promise of service when needed.

Some time later, when he decided which suppliers were to be favoured with his orders, he ran up some alarming accounts. In the meantime, he repeatedly sent one complaint after another to the suppliers. As accounts departments function independently of others, he was a regular recipient of bills and statements but, of course, he made no attempt to settle any of them on the grounds that the goods supplied were defective. It was a matter of applied psychology. No firm which thinks that it might be in the wrong will press for payment until the wrong is righted, and the game can go on for twelve months or more. A clever man like Wally was able to rattle through his sub-contracts and then think about his overdue bills. But this did not mean that he was about to settle. Far from it.

About two years after he started playing this game of ducks and drakes he acquired the services of a very clever solicitor. His letters began to appear in the file with some frequency. Once more Wally's complaints were put, this time in legal jargon. Bad deliveries, poor quality, short quantities, not up to specification, these and other get-outs spattered the correspondence. Then one firm did take legal action to try and get payment of nearly £5,000, applying Order 14 of the rules of the Supreme Court. All the papers seemed to be in order, including a notarized statement by the firm. Somewhere along the line a legal quibble was raised, holding up the action for three months, after which it did look as though Wally had reached the end of the road and would have to pay up.

Almost on the eve of the final hearing Wally apparently made an offer to the firm, suggesting that they call a halt to the legal proceedings. In return, he would pay the bill off in instalments over an agreed period. Studying the terms of the offer, I could not help smiling at this audacity, especially after finding that it took three more months to agree on the terms of the payments. On the brink once more, and no doubt well aware that the firm would not want to go to law yet again, Wally told them that he wanted a deduction for all the inconvenience he had suffered. On top of this he threatened to take legal action for the loss of one of his contracts. This did not wash but the firm was forced to accept some of his conditions.

Although business is a large affair and it is spread all over the country, word does get round quickly, and it travels not only through trade associations but also the representatives of companies. The clever fraud works quickly and clears a small profit or else he builds up a tortuous network of companies which is virtually impenetrable. The 'long firm' fraud is in the second category, and it is so well organized that it is now being pulled time after time with success.

Running the long firm fraud calls for a certain amount of capital, because it must be financed to the tune of £5,000 or more. One gang which operates in the north of England and in Scotland has a 'finance branch' in London which uses other types of fraud to establish a new long firm swindle as and when required. Everything is planned and phased in such a way that the long firm operators can estimate practically to the day when they will be able to start up in business. While the 'base party' labours to raise the money, the long firm merchants start visiting wholesale warehouses to deliver the preliminary spiel. This is generally to the effect that they will shortly be starting a business in the area and they have called to see whether they might open an account. At the same time money is deposited with a bank in the district. Money filters through from the London end with some regularity, quickly building up to the agreed ceiling of £5,000. It is customary to use one man with the right sort of presence and patter to front the operation and impart an air of reliability. Anybody who requires trade reference receives the address of the London operation, which uses a variety of letter-heads, all of them wholly convincing. Before the war the racket concentrated on textiles, but it has now shifted to consumer durables, such as washing machines, electric kettles, gardening equipment and occasional furniture. The criterion is that everything must be portable, and the goods are carefully chosen so as to appeal to newlyweds and others who want something which looks good and is moderately priced. The real target is not the consumer but the wholesaler.

The long firm organization now starts trading, and they go on doing this for up to three years. During the first year more accounts are opened with other wholesalers, using the references of one for the other. In the final investigation it will transpire that only one person, the credit controller or the director of the original firm of wholesalers, actually saw a reference from outside the immediate circle. The gang is clever in its planning, because for eighteen months to two years the accounts will be paid as soon as a statement is received. That mysterious element called credit reliability is being built up with wholesalers and bank, but what the wholesalers cannot know is that a certain percentage of the goods are being sold from a rented shop several miles away. One gang even opened its own small wholesale warehouse to supply retailers. All goods are sold below the catalogue price. This seemingly foolhardy move helps to create a cash flow to keep pace with the bills.

Now for the final devastating phase.

One gang interested the director of a wholesale suppliers in taking 'shares' with their firm, and he put up the large sum of £25,000 which, of course, vanished overnight. Other devices for quick money making based on the firm's reputation are used. The more orthodox long firm now surveys the wholesalers with which it has accounts in good standing. If it is being done on a big scale, as many as 100 wholesalers in different parts of the country may be involved. The long firm knows what suppliers' stocks amount to, because this sort of knowledge is easy to come by in casual conversation with departmental managers. In the final swoop the gang will put in orders for large quantities of goods, such as several hundred washing machines, a thousand electric kettles, dozens of canteens of cutlery, knitted goods and other garments by the bale. The unsuspecting wholesalers prepare the goods, which will be picked up by hired vans in a matter of hours. The operation is so timed that the accounts will not fall due for at least one month. At the same time, the orders are spread out over so many wholesalers that no single firm will suspect what is going on.

The obvious happens. The gang has furniture vans waiting elsewhere and in a matter of hours the goods are on their way to London, Liverpool, Manchester and other centres, where they are quickly sold to people who are, in reality, fences. For their part, the fences keep the stuff in locked warehouses, filtering them out to dealers who are not too particular where or how they buy their stock.

What does an average long firm fraud actually yield? Disregarding the need for the fairly large operating capital, the returns can be phenomenal. A group of five men who spent more than three years planning and executing such a fraud cleared three-quarters of a million pounds. None of them were caught.

The only man I ever knew who was a long firm fraud specialist was Suleman Setty. While he was ostensibly a car dealer in Golders Green in north London, most of his money came from long firm operations in carpets and floor coverings. Setty was not a very pleasant man, he had too many grudges which he carried round with him, and he was always trying to push his hot goods. It was ironical that Donald Hume, who pleaded guilty to a charge of being an accessory to the murder, rolled Setty's body up in a carpet, carted it down the stairs above the shop where Setty lived in some sort of squalid splendour, and then drove to the airfield where he had a light plane. It was claimed that he flew Setty's body over the Essex marshes after cutting it up, and dropped pieces of the long firm operator here and there.

You might feel that a lot of very hard work is done by practitioners of such frauds as these, and you would be right. In my experience, when men are involved in a major project, they do work incredibly hard if the reward is big enough. I have known several people who were only too willing to go to prison for a few years if they could come out to live the rest of their lives on the thousands of pounds couped in a big scheme. Just how much this sum might be is variable, but £50,000 and upwards is adequate for most people. At a time when our prisons are bursting and practically all cells designed originally for one prisoner are accommodating two people, and about 1,000 new prisoners arrive monthly, it is not entirely beyond possibility that conmen and other frauds might in future be regarded as relatively harmless in comparison with the violent criminals. Other forms of punishment could be devised for conmen and frauds, and a hefty fine could be a purgative, despite the fact that the extent of the fine cannot equal the amount which the swindler has accumulated. But we have to face the fact that most conmen are never caught, and this applies particularly to the world of industrial espionage. I wrote about this in Chapter One, but more can be said at this point about the *modus operandi*, the actual method of obtaining detailed information which has a market value.

Many of the highly skilled men are the disgruntled men of our time, and this applies particularly to chartered engineers, research and development personnel, industrial chemists. Under a Socialist government they found themselves less well paid than, say, ordinary shopfloor operatives, who have no real skills and have not spent years studying for professional qualifications. They are the focus of industrial spying. But before going on to consider exactly how trade secrets can be acquired at a low price and sold for a tremendous profit, it would be a good idea to look first at the whole question of industrial intelligence, which plays an important role in the national economy. From the outside looking in anybody can be forgiven for seeing in the Them/Us conflict a struggle like a war. It has its leaders and its troops, and each separate action is not what it seems but part of a whole. Most of the industrial stoppages—during the first four months of 1970 no less than 3,096,000 days were lost through strikes as compared with 4,313,000 in the same period of 1962—were for money rather than an improvement in working conditions. It is while negotiations are in progress that the pattern of hope and counter-hope begins to assert itself, and it is as though the negotiators have some inside knowledge about the point at which management will begin to agree. In this sense such negotiations are not negotiations at all but simple banditry in view of the fact that the unions know in advance how much money is in the purse. This may baffle some industrialists but it is clear that the unions are now utilizing some form of industrial intelligence. While some union negotiators may be men of integrity, there is nevertheless a murky undercurrent which could not withstand deep investigation.

In March 1969 there was a meeting at Sheffield of the Seventh National Congress of the Institute for Workers' Control, when a resolution was passed to form, or establish, an advisory bureau to link shop stewards during industrial disputes to a source of technical assistance when it becomes necessary to scrutinize audits, company reports and other material to which the workers do not normally have access and which they would not, in any case, understand.

In 1969 the British Labour government announced a significant aspect of industrial policy, to enable the workers' councils to have access to company records. Since that time there has been a build-up of concerted action in certain industries, particularly in the automobile industry, and during a weekend meeting held on 13/14 September 1969, and organized by the International Car Workers' Conference under the aegis of the Institute for Workers' Control, held at Coventry and attended by key workers' representatives from Yugoslavia, France and Italy, various resolutions were passed including the formation of a co-ordinating committee of research workers, officials and shop stewards, who were charged with drafting plans for workers' control of the industry itself.

At least one union is known to have employed a private detective agency to ferret out certain items of information about a company and the salaries paid to its senior executives. The fee paid to the detective agency by the union was £5,000.

Industrial spying obviously goes on in all directions. The aviation and shipbuilding industries are subject to constant scrutiny by foreign governments. The rapid industrial growth of countries like Germany and Japan are due not so much to their own know-how but to the extent of their industrial spying networks.

There are several international agencies which do nothing else but acquire what can loosely be called 'trade secrets'. While some of these secrets are quite small, others are large enough to warrant agency fees of more than £12,000 a year in cases where a flow of information is required by the client. This most certainly applied to the Anglo-French Concorde programme. The bigger the project, the easier the acquisition of information. Concorde was spread out over dozens of plants in Britain and France, and in one case the client was said to have paid £50,000 down to the espionage organizers, followed by monthly cheques of £6,000 or more, depending upon the amount of information supplied. Exactly how the information was collected must be obvious to anybody who is versed in the techniques of industrial espionage, where every man has his price. With so large a catchment area, it was not difficult to affix the 'taps' from which a flow of valuable information would run. The result is practically history. The Russian TU144 is already airborne and observers have said that it looks exactly like the Concorde. This is not to imply that Russian technology lags behind that of the West, but anybody in research and development knows that the earliest stages of a project are the costliest. From the point of view of the espionage client, this is the most important material to procure. It is the know-how that matters, and the target is the research and development man. It costs an average £10,000 a year to maintain a senior research man in industry. These men and their assistants are the focus of attention. Within industrial spying and commercial espionage there are ten men at the top. All of them are incredibly wealthy.

The office of one of the spymasters is in the provinces. I went there on a blind errand, simply to dangle a hook with some bait. The address was passed to me by an acquaintance. They were expecting me, the man and his wife, and they turned out to be very English and very hospitable as they conducted me to a somewhat stodgy hotel near the office where we sat in the lounge. The wife poured the tea, said that the cakes and sandwiches looked stale, and then relapsed into an expectant silence broken curtly by her husband, who asked my business. I said that my client was interested in Rolls-Royce at Derby and a number of aero engine firms. It was simply a matter of knowing which research programmes were going forward and which were putting programmes into abeyance. We were particularly interested in Rolls-Royce, however, in view of their application for a government loan of about £20 million.

He named a fee and said that he could supply a file on Rolls-Royce within a month to six weeks.

One does not, of course, clinch an offer on the basis of a cup of hotel tea.

'It's a very small job,' he said persuasively. 'I've got men on the spot all the time. Would £10,000 suit your client?' When I said that it sounded reasonable, he suddenly beamed. 'Well, good. And if you want anything from overseas, don't forget us. We have associates in all the main centres.'

The information which he and his friends can provide is practically limitless and it is of interest to both technological and commercial sectors, including the figures for tenders which are about to be presented; analyses of market developments by companies; plans for takeovers and mergers, and so on. The most closely guarded secrets about a company's financial position can be discovered within hours, given an informant such as a junior board member or a company accountant who can be bought. Such people can sometimes be won over by offering a fairly large sum of money or the promise of a job elsewhere at a higher salary. There are men who make a good living as scouts, seeking out weak and vulnerable companies and acquiring inside information about their trading position, their under-capitalization and then compiling a dossier, which is peddled discreetly to other companies which are in the takeover business. The rightness or the wrongness of this kind of strategy could be discussed at length, but the ethical side of it is outside our terms of reference.

To conclude this picture of an industrial society in which it is possible not only to acquire confidential information but also the companies themselves, here is a story about one of the men who traded dossiers on companies. He had his eye on a certain company which was the subject of a dossier. It was not very big or important, but it did hold a key position in plastics moulding by the extrusion process. The bulk of the business came from sub-contracting to the motor industry. Having spent months tapping various technical and commercial sources, he was finally defeated on two counts. He needed more information about certain points concerning appropriations. Without these items he could not hope to sell the dossier to the client he had in mind.

In the end he reversed the entire process and met the managing director and chairman of the company. In a convincing tale, he said that he had discovered that their company was in a parlous state. To prove it he produced a doctored version of the dossier. After some private discussion, they were profuse in their appreciation and not only offered him a cheque in return for some information about the plastics industry but also a position as a security officer in the firm. After starting work for them he was soon able to acquire the elusive information and, in due course, he completed the dossier and sold it, as originally planned, to a competitor.

The main outflow of information from most firms is the telephone switchboard. It would be a simple-minded intelligence man who overlooked the possibility of using this prime source. I once knew two women who did very well indeed, because both were trained telephonists, both spoke several languages and they were highly efficient. Exactly how they discovered the possibility of selling information is not quite clear, but they were approached by a man in the industrial espionage game, who said that he could augment their meagre wages. They worked only for firms which used two telephone operators, and so were able to install a miniature tape recorder to make a permanent note of interesting conversations. The reels of tape were posted daily to a certain address.

Without in any way reflecting on the high standard of many employment agencies it should, however, be noted that when a girl who works for an industrial spying organization wants to obtain employment in a firm where information is waiting to be picked up, she can generally do so by utilizing the services of an agency, particularly an agency which supplies temporaries. A girl with good qualifications and appearance can pick her jobs if she works as a temporary.

As a general rule industrial spying is not simply a matter of slipping an individual haphazardly into a firm and simply hoping that odds and ends might be picked up, although there was the case of a charwoman/tea lady who had a spectacular success by collecting the contents of the managing director's wastepaper basket and passing them over. It is not always as easy as that, especially in technical matters. If a man cannot be planted in a firm, there are other methods, which may take a little longer but are still capable of producing results. It is not even necessary to plant anyone on the premises. This is how it works.

The specialist in this method is middle-aged, extremely well educated and he spent more than ten years in industry, mainly is a managerial or executive position. It is unnecessary to analyse the reasons which took him into his present work. As he pointed out, he had always been interested in security work from both ends. He is likeable even if his conversation is on the guarded side, and there are times when it dawns on you that he is actually saying nothing at all and simply filling a silence. After some months of mutual trust he began to talk to me, apologizing that he is careful by nature. When you have sweated for all these years, bought a house worth £15,000 at current prices, sent your children to good schools and taken your holidays aboard a chartered yacht, you do have a tendency to be careful.

'The real point is the complexity of industry, isn't it? Just look at a firm like I.C.I. with 100,000 people on the U.K. payroll—and about 7,000 of them are graduates—and plants everywhere with heavy concentrations in the north-west and on Teesside.' He is the proverbial walking encyclopaedia when it comes to companies, able to give you all the data on them, from the name of the chairman through to the recruitment policy and how much they spend per head on finding top talent.

'The demand for information is insatiable. In order to satisfy this appetite for facts and figures, you have to attract customers. The more difficult thing is getting people who do have the information to come to you.'

'How safe is this information gathering?'

'Quite safe. You see, no firm would want it to be known that they have gone to the length of engaging in this kind of strategy. I do wish people would stop referring to it as industrial spying or espionage. There's a distasteful connotation to it, and I think it should be called industrial intelligence or something of that kind, because that's what it is, and nobody really gets hurt, except some of the shareholders now and then, although a chap might occasionally get the sack. But nobody gets his throat cut. It's relatively harmless, especially when a big firm is involved. They can afford it.'

'What about the ethics of it?'

'That's an old-fashioned word nowadays. If you knew what went on in many of these companies, you couldn't mention ethics, especially in companies with lots of subsidiaries where the executives are always gunning for one another. A director once told me that a spirit of competition within a group was healthy, and he obviously didn't know much about his own executives. I've never met such an unhappy bunch of men. A lot of the theory about the science of management is hot air, you know. There isn't a job in management that can't be mastered inside a month. No, I mean that. Of course, I'm technical these days, so it doesn't apply to my firm. Yes, very technical. That's where the money is, that's where everything has to start . . .

'I've got four partners. We started concentrating on chemical engineering four years ago quite by accident, because up to that time we'd thrown a pretty wide net, especially in mechanical engineering, and we'd done enormously well, especially with the Germans. We certainly earned our money. Have you ever been to Wallsend, near Newcastle? It's damned near the end of the world as far as I'm concerned. Anyway, we set up a smart office down there, just to keep an eye on shipbuilding. It was all very clumsy and obvious, but these were the early days, and perhaps we lacked know-how, but we did pull through. There was one bit of unpleasantness with a chap in a drawing office, but we got him off the hook and settled him with a firm in Scotland. I think he's still there . . .

'Well, that's water under the bridge and not very interesting. About a year later we decided to change the shape of the firm. Forced into it really, because nuclear engineering was on the up and up, though there didn't seem to be much in it for us. I thought we should close down for a bit. We could afford it. Then one of our chaps started going into the remote stuff, especially chemical engineering. There was a lot going on in synthesis and causation, compounds and that sort of stuff, and a hell of a lot of it was connected with the plastics industry. In our business we always invest a great deal of time and money in our own research to look into feasibility, so we did a huge study of the industries where chemical engineering had some link, and after that we split up for a time, trying to find out something about the market for information. It really was a cracker! Nearly every firm we approached was absolutely avid for anything we could sell them. We did this part of it by starting a dummy firm which purported to be in the business of publishing scientific and industrial abstracts. It looked very impressive. We sent questionnaires to five hundred firms, and there wasn't much doubt that the entirely mythical service we were proposing would be very useful to any firm. Then we sat down and evaluated all the replies and made quite a few useful contacts that way.'

'But what was the real purpose of all this?'

'Ground work, sheer ground work. Plus the contacts, of course, because those mythical abstracts brought us in close touch with research and development boys. We even wined and dined some of them. Surprising how easily a lot of them talked about their work. By this time we'd got a qualified chemical engineer on our own staff, and he told us they dropped some damned interesting stuff over food and drink.'

'What did you do after that?'

'Do? Well, the usual thing. We started another firm, and this time it was in manpower selection. I don't want to go into our reasons, except that people are the key to information and people are easy to get at. Round about that time we got hold of our first client. It was only a small firm, but they'd got a lot of money, and they wanted to break into synthetic resins. This was a year or two before synthetic resins really got going, although research had been going on for years. Anyway, the one thing they couldn't afford was a full-time research chemist, although they had a part-time consultant. What they were after was a link in the chain. The method we used is much the same as we use now—'

'You wouldn't like to talk about it, would you?'

'I don't mind. Anyway, we are going out of business soon, so it won't matter. But I'm damned if I'll give you the full picture. . . . However, you might not know this, but whenever you want to know about an area of absolute specialization, you can easily find out almost exactly how many leading men there are working in that area. Would you be surprised to know that in some fields of advanced research, there are only five or six men working? It's quite true. Of course, it's very easy to find out where they are through professional associations and other ways. There's an association for practically everything nowadays. So . . . what what one does is dangle a bait in front of the little fishes. Sounds callous, doesn't it? It depends how you look at it. The bait takes the form of an advertisement through our executive and placement agency. Actually, as an agency we are quite well known and we do a lot of entirely legitimate business, so it looks quite above board. The advertisement is carefully drafted, and it is intended to catch their eyes, because it describes the very job they are doing. The difference is that the salary is about two or three times what they are receiving at the moment. Naturally, most of them are tempted and so several of them write for further details.'

'I don't quite understand how you can be sure they'll see the advertisement.'

'We plaster it around—Sunday papers, weeklies, all the scientific journals, the association journals and so on and so forth, and in any case we always send a copy anonymously. It's a funny thing, but I've never known any of them question the origin.'

'And what happens then?'

'Well, as a rule they write and express a cautious interest, and we invite them along for an exploratory interview, all expenses paid. It doesn't matter if a man is coming from the other end of the country or whether it costs fifty quid to get him into the office, because what we are after is potentially worth several thousand pounds. It's ludicrously simple to get them to discuss their work, and so long as you know what you want to get out of him and you're a qualified man in that particular line, it's easy. When all's said and done, they are curious about the job and the idea of getting a position with better facilities and a house and a free car—those are the inducements—well, imagine how you'd feel. It's like coming to the end of the rainbow. When the brain drain was in full flood we were offering positions in America that had Prime Minister's salaries attached to them plus a villa in Florida and all the rest of the nonsense, and people really believed it. So in this sort of atmosphere, talking about the work which you are doing at the moment doesn't seem very detrimental to your firm, especially if you start thinking you'll be leaving soon anyway. Technical fellows are pretty childlike as a rule. Half of them have never heard about industrial intelligence. I remember one fellow who actually wrote down a lot of formulae when our interviewer challenged him, and another one had all his lab reports photostated for us. In the usual way, though, we have a tape recorder going in the drawer of the desk and a mike under the inkstand.'

'So they don't hear any more from you after this interview?'

'We keep them dangling for a time to make it look really convincing. Quite a few times we have chaps up for a second or even a third interview when our client has wanted more detailed information. But you can't go beyond three interviews, because it does begin to look fishy. In the end we just let them down gently and tell them the job's gone. They're often remarkably grateful for all the attention we've given to their application.'

During the last five years the organization has grown so that it now forms part of a European network with centres in Germany, Italy, France and London, and much of the technical information finds its way across the Atlantic or to the Iron Curtain countries. The financial turnover cannot be estimated. Sufficient to say that the man to whom I talked had an annual income in excess of that of the Governor of the Bank of England. In May 1970 it was revealed that the Governor of the Bank of England was in receipt of £25,000 a year.

The incongruous thing about fraud or white-collar crime on this scale is that it is not, in Britain at least, a crime in itself, although some segments of it may infringe the law. The placement agency misrepresents the facts because no job actually exists. On the side of the applicant there may be an offence when he removes what may be company property in the shape of research reports and other material, including samples. It has often been suggested that industrial espionage on this scale should be made into a legal offence carrying extremely high penalties on the grounds that it is an offence against property. But who is to investigate? The Fraud Squad? It is doubtful whether they could cope, good though they may be when it comes to City crime. The companies which feel most vulnerable employ counter-espionage operators, and it is perhaps the only thing they can do at the moment. But industrial counter-espionage is as much open to abuse as the private detective business. It has often been said that a private enquiry agency can be started up by a saint or a scoundrel without let or hindrance from local authority, police or parliament. When it comes to industrial counter-espionage the situation is the same, although it is still a very small profession in terms of numbers, and all the operatives know one another, so there is little chance of fraud creeping into the preventative sector without some form of vigilante action taking place. The weakest member of the set-up is the commercial or industrial company itself, because it all too often aids and abets the intelligence operators by refusing to prosecute, even when grounds exist for doing so. A flourishing and healthy company prefers to avoid this type of unsavoury publicity, especially if it is a public company with thousands of investors. The good name of a firm is worth far more than retribution against one offender and several ugly splashes of national publicity. Besides—and we have to face this fact—there is always a chance that if a company does bring an action or has to agree to a police prosecution, the accused may 'know where the body is buried' and he will dig it up in court out of sheer revenge. When it comes to the crunch, every company has something to hide, and we cannot easily forget Edwin Sutherland's *White Collar Criminality* (American Sociological Review 5 : 1–2 February 1940) in which he discovered that the 200 biggest manufacturing, mining and mercantile corporations in America were all guilty of offences under six different headings, from misrepresentation in advertising and trade restraint to financial fraud and violation of trust, and including 'infringement of patents, trade marks and copyright'. Industrial espionage often falls into the last category, and in her *Crime in Modern Society* (Harper, 1952) Mabel A. Elliott cites a firm which sold equipment ranging from electric fans to cream separators, violating no less than 19 patent rights. She also mentions firms which engage in a more devious racket: 'In addition to these bona fide cases of patent infringement certain firms engaged in patent manipulation, securing patents for minor alterations in existing patents in order to obtain the right to initiate damage suits in case of infringements. This practice has become a virtual racket in the major mechanical and electrical industries. Certain clever engineers take out patents which make minor improvements on existing patents. Principles involved in these alterations are more or less bound to occur to other inventors and the holder of the patent initiates a suit as soon as slight changes are introduced by the other manufacturer. Such infringement suits may literally have the law on their side and yet be a form of coercion which amounts to a definite restraint of trade. Many inventors make fortunes out of such suits.'

Such games are played in Britain, too, and many a company holds inventions with the sole intention of using them to make trouble with other companies when the time is right. Other corporate pastimes include the hobby of Cheating the Income Tax. As these words are being written a garment trade director is being told to pay £11,000 in back-tax, accumulated over the years by clever book-keeping. He leaves court claiming that he is ruined, because he saved nothing and spent it all. An obvious case of bad planning, whereas the fraudulent operator will stash his loot away abroad and then leave the country where he can enjoy his gains in peace. Some may pay nominal tax on an income which can withstand investigation, but the Inland Revenue thinks that £150 million is 'won' by tax frauds every year and the figure is still rising, encouraged by the cramping economic climate of Britain. After all, it costs a firm about £6 a head per week to employ people when social insurance and other dues are paid. In a small business which employs about 50 people, this comes to £300 a week, or £14,400 a year. We need not go into the matter of wages and the escalation of overheads, but it is obvious to anybody in business that this encourages fraud. Enough to say that, though a High Court judge once said that 'Every man is entitled if he can to order his affairs so that the tax . . . is less than it otherwise would be. If he succeeds in ordering them so as to secure this result then, however unappreciative the Commissioners of Inland Revenue or fellow taxpayers may be of his ingenuity, he cannot be compelled to pay an increased tax'. There is, of course, a world of difference between legal avoidance and illegal evasion of tax, but this is a fact which seems to have evaded the notice of the twenty million or more who pay income tax.

The kingpin is, of course, the accountant, and ever since income tax became a burning topic, he has become more and more important. The man who advises on tax avoidance is much sought after, and so is the accountant who can create an opportunity for evasion.

The man I have in mind was made redundant without any warning after twenty years with the same firm and, as an unqualified commercial accountant, he found himself on the end of the dole queue in a depressed area, reflecting that the golden handshake which he had just received would not go very far. He owned a house, his son and daughter were both married, and his wife was dead. The sensation of being alone was not one which he could stomach very easily. The dole queue moved forward a few inches and then stopped again, and he looked at the faces of the other men and felt alien to them. He must get away from this depressing atmosphere. In the next few weeks he attempted to get a job, but he was defeated at every turn. They wanted a qualified man, whereas all he could offer was experience and it counted for nothing. In such a situation a man will often turn inwards on himself. He remembered his own father, a self-employed general dealer in a coastal resort. He had always seemed happy, contented, and he was never short of money. But self-employment then and self-employment now were two different things. Despite some misgivings, he decided to start a small mail order firm, selling tools and gadgets. To his surprise it did very well, and he even made some profit. Put in these terms, it sounds very simple and, according to the man who did it, the actual making of money, from £2,000 to £150,000 in less than five years, was simple, and it was merely a matter of buying right and selling quickly for fairly small profits. In this time he did practically all the work himself, enjoying every moment of it.

When the gloom of income tax spread across the sunny sky and it was obvious that up to one-third of the profits might be claimed, an element of doubt crept into his life. Obviously, he had to do something. His first action was to start a second company to act on paper as a stockholder to sell merchandise to the first company. This did create a useful tax absorption device. But soon this company, too, was showing a profit, and so a new company was started to administer the other two, and here again, it was a 'paper company'. It created a tax loss. The snowball was now rolling along nicely and he was picking up useful tax avoidance dodges as he went along. In time he ran out of names for directors in his own family and resorted to making them up. By the time he had more than forty companies registered, the taxman was beginning to take notice, because the man behind it did not seem to draw any salary, merely odd sums of money as expenses. When the heat was on, he finally formed another company with one solitary purpose, to employ him at a salary so nominal that it did not attract any tax liability.

Sitting in the lounge of his house, I could not help laughing as he pressed more brandy on me. He looked so neat, clean and tidy and so innocent that it was almost unbelievable that he had beaten the tax man at his own game by what sounded like a very simple expedient.

'Tax,' he said, 'it's a thing everybody hates yet nobody does anything about. If all the effort we spend talking about it could be used constructively, I'm sure we could put it down like a sick dog. After all, it's more than a century since the Chancellor introduced income tax and said it would last only seven years, and it's still with us. We've now arrived at the point where there isn't a tax inspector in the country who can give you a snap answer to a complicated question about your income tax affairs. It's not so long ago that the Inland Revenue people were threatening to strike because they couldn't keep up with amendments and revisions and all the work of administering it. The Inland Revenue is like a thundering great elephant and the taxpayers are the midges. But when it comes to business, why should they tax profits? It's tax on sweat and brains. The way I've done it, I've piled up so much company liability that the taxman can't refuse the claims, even if he does feel it's a bit of a fiddle or, to put it more properly, an avoidance. You can't blame people, you can only blame the government, the economy. What right do they have to our money? If they can't manage the country at an economical level, they ought to be chucked out.'

In tax matters the best adviser is the ex-tax inspector turned private accountant. Many disgruntled tax inspectors who have 'gone over to the other side' make about £8,000 a year minimum, and they spend most of their time, as one of them told me, 'hauling people out of the fertilizer'. The trouble is that most of the clients arrive too late, when the tax inspector has their file permanently on his desk. As soon as the inspector gets a smell of any irregularity, the chase is on. But how does it all start? The first point at which the inspector knows anything about your affairs is when the tax return itself is examined. In Britain, at least, we are now at a point where your tax affairs follow you round, and even if you go to an entirely new area, the tax inspector is bound to ask where you lived previously so that he can send for your file. Nobody appears out of the blue unless he happens to be a refugee. When people complain about the invasion of privacy, they overlook how much the tax inspector knows about them, and a lot of this begins with the statutory obligation of the banks, Post Office, Savings Banks and Trustee Savings Banks to report the names of the accounts holders who receive more than £15 interest per year. It does not take a lot of capital to produce £15 per year, but you can, of course, spread out deposits and get away with it. I did work this out once and it seemed to be possible to salt away about £12,000 without any interference.

An accountant said: 'The Inland Revenue has powers to look into all kinds of matters. For instance, in many offices an inspector will read all the business news in local newspapers, and if a local business man has been over-zealous in his wish for publicity and announced that he has done a deal or bought a rare picture or started an investment company or anything at all involving money, a clipping goes into that man's file and some time in the future we will see if it is reflected in his tax returns. If it is not so reflected, then the Enquiry Branch may take over and the real crunch starts'. This accountant was a Civil Servant, anxious to leave tax gathering and start up on his own.

The practised tax evader ensures that he receives his money in cash from sources which are practically impossible to trace. Once he has the cash, he spreads it around, often in several dozen small bank accounts under a variety of different names. American and other foreign banks with branches throughout Britain are not too particular about references for new customers, and this is particularly useful where the individual requires credit cards under other names and uses accommodation addresses. One of the most accomplished conmen I have ever met had to pull out a wad of credit cards under many different names to verify his current identity. 'Twelve,' he grinned. 'I'm twelve different people. Tomorrow may be different.' The Inland Revenue cannot hope to keep track of such people, and even if they did pin one down, how could they reconcile multiple personalities with the tax liability of a single individual? The twelve-sided man kindly did some sums for me, because I was interested to know how much on average each of these entirely mythical personalities made in a typical year. It came out, conservatively, at about £3,000 each, making a total of £36,000, tax free. Some of it came from insurance.

But insurance is not what it was and today it is necessary to use considerable ingenuity to beat the assessors and adjustors at their own game. One method used by the twelve-sided man is to take a factory premises on short lease and then stock it with used printing equipment, which can be picked up fairly cheaply. Small rotary presses, flat-bed machines, guillotines and other pieces of machinery are accumulated until he is able to call in a broker/valuer who is prepared to sell the lot on commission. An estimate is prepared which shows a figure somewhat in excess of the real value. A retainer is paid on this basis, governed by the estimated value. Next, the operator shops round for an insurance policy. In the provinces there is more shilly-shallying than in London.

'You might not believe this, but I've insured warehouses in London without the insurers even bothering to come round and see them, but in the sticks—oh, brother, they really go into it, you've no idea. They've probably got more time on their hands. Not that they know what they're looking at.'

The insurance valuation of the goods is, of necessity, higher than the valuer's figure. Insurance companies are interested only in the degree of risk and the security of the building rather than the actual contents.

He put his credit cards away. 'Then we have a burn up,' he said simply. 'I like a daytime blaze myself. Looks more convincing if there's one or two blokes on the premises. We get temporary mechanics in, stripping the junk down, cleaning it up. The fire starts almost before their very eyes. Little bomb gadget full of chlorate. Goes off puff, then it's a case of everybody out!'

The economics of the operation are as follows: cost of second-hand machinery up to approximately £2,500. Rental of warehouse approximately £15 per week for no more than three weeks. Wages of four mechanics for 14 days £100–£150. Insurance coverage to £15,000. Of course, the fire must be sufficiently widespread to reduce the machinery to scrap, but this is not difficult to arrange for a practised fire-raiser.

Insurance fraud cannot be practised on a continuous basis, and for that reason is the province only of the top professionals. Naturally, every conman dreams of a method of making money which will provide a continuous income and apparent respectability. Cheap common rackets are distinguished by their short-term prospects, and while it is possible to make from £500 to £1,000 a week on this circuit, many of the operators who have been in the get-rich-quick game for years profess to be fed up with it. They want something steady. It does sound vaguely ludicrous when you appreciate the fact that even the minnows in the game can produce as much as £20,000 of loose change to finance new ventures. The picture of the impoverished conman is anachronistic.

Some conmen actually know very little about finance and the manipulation of money. All they know is that they want money. One man who comes to mind was approaching his late middle age when he started worrying about the future. His wife, part Syrian and part English Jewess, finally rounded on him, fed up to the back teeth with his moping and air of uncertainty. What did he want, to be respectable or something? He eyed her reproachfully. What was respectability? They had money, house, car, kids, so he should worry? No, it was something deeper than that, he murmured, maybe like a male menopause . . .

Pop-eyed, unable to believe her ears, she threw back her head and laughed so much that sweat ran down her broad forehead and into her eyes. She was practically hysterical. At the age of 39 she was one of those voluptuous, heavy-thighed and deepbusted women, entirely materialistic and yet still managing to be darkly mysterious. The one thing which she personally detested was anything that disturbed the home. But this menopause stuff —she collapsed on a settee, still laughing as he slammed out of the house for one of his brooding walks in the park.

When she met her father, a widower with an estate business, she mentioned it to him. He, too, could not help laughing, although at the back of his mind he remembered the marriage and how he had wished that his only daughter was marrying a real man. Of course, the fellow had made a lot of money out of various deals, he was a clever boy, but so pale and weak, no personality. However, money was money, so why rabbit on about it?

Father and daughter paid their weekly visit to Fortnums for tea, and as he slowly mashed up a gateau he confessed that he, too, was worried about his age. Very soon he intended selling up his business. With this government things were getting harder and harder. She was flabbergasted and pointed out that he had spent thirty years, building up the estate business and now here he was, wanting to get out. What was the matter with everybody these days? Leaning over the table, she suggested that he get together with her husband and talk things over and maybe together they could work things out. It would be good for everybody. Her father agreed, remarking that she ought to have been born a boy . . .

After talking to a few of his friends father called on his son-in-law and offered a proposition. Together, they could raise a lot of money, right? And together they could start lending money, right? The son-in-law began to look doubtful. Not so right, he said, because you needed a licence and the police were very hot on money lending. Poppa shut him up. Naw-naw, just listen, eh? They would start a building society—well, anyway, something called a building society. This was not so difficult. Call it a trust or something like that. Now, just like any other building society, they would lend money, but not on primary mortgages. They would lend up to £500 to anybody with collateral or some security, but the best security would be a house, bricks and mortar. And the interest, said Poppa, who had looked into it from top to bottom, would be anything from 18 per cent up to about 34 per cent. That would be the true interest rate.

So Poppa and his son-in-law did start the company and it prospered under the cloak of the 'second mortgage' offer to householders. They appointed a nationwide network of broker/

agents to make it look real, although it could have been run on a mail order basis. The scheme was designed and drafted by a solicitor and a retired banker for a large fee, and, as Poppa happily exclaimed after examining it: 'When you buy gold, you pay the price of gold!'

This was no confidence trick. It was quite above board, because the clients were given every opportunity of consulting their own solicitors. Not that many seemed to do so for the simple reason that they were anxious to get their hands on the money at a time when bank borrowing was severely restricted. The real profits came from several sources, including the so-called administration charge of five per cent of the total loan; the surveyor's fee for examining the property which was to be used as security, and this could be anywhere from £7 to £30, and, finally, the legal fees of £40 to £60. On a seven-year loan the interest was 23 per cent. Within hours of the first advertisements appearing in the national press, enquiries flooded into the London office and, going through some of the letters, Poppa grunted: 'Some of these fellows, they'd pledge their wives for a couple of hundred quid.'

So great was the demand that it was decided to appoint brokers, or agents, throughout the country with the inducement of a high commission on successful loans negotiated. It looked rosy and it was rosy until the business sections of some of the Sunday newspapers started taking an interest in Poppa and his son-in-law as a result of one or two unfortunate cases. For instance, one client refused to pay £40 for cancelling an agreement for a £3,000 loan. Some nosey parker appeared on television to tell everybody that £200 interest on £500 over seven years was too high. It seemed that everybody objected to paying contract fees and legal expenses. Poppa shrugged off the national furore and cut down the advertisements, and started to operate a little more quietly but still within the law. He had by now made a borrowing arrangement with a merchant bank, who required him to use reasonable means to make defaulters pay up before they went into action, and so Poppa installed what he called his 'get tough' department consisting of two young and ambitious lawyers, and already it was doing well, hitting the bad payers so hard that they landed in the county courts. In four years he had 360 houses throughout the country, all legally acquired and all rented out. In a number of cases he permitted the original owner-borrowers to stay on, and if the rent was a little higher than he would have paid on his mortgage repayments, well, that was life, eh?

Since Poppa and his son-in-law went in the second mortgage game, this is a business which has mushroomed all over the country. At the last count in 1970 the borrowers owed £50 million, but in the event of further inflation it is liable to shoot up to £200 million. The second mortgage brokers, while doubtless legitimate in their dealings, are nevertheless uncontrolled as far as interest rates and extra service charges are concerned, and nothing short of legislation will halt their progress. They will obviously continue to flourish within the inflated British economy, which was second only to Japan for the period 1963–1970. Countries below Britain for the same period include France, Italy, America and West Germany. As we have agreed elsewhere in this book, graft and corruption will flourish in a certain type of financial climate.

In May 1970 the citizens of Bradford, Yorkshire, heard strong rumours of bribes paid for corporation contracts. Twenty firms were said to be involved, and so many big names were mixed up in it over a period of seven years that Bradford city police handed the investigation over to the West Riding police at Wakefield to ensure complete impartiality. The £5,000 a year head architect of the corporation was sacked and so was his secretary. One man who had been to prison in connection with the case said: 'I have heard both in my job and in prison, that palm greasing of local and public authority officials in order to get contracts is widespread in this country.'

Where, then, is an area which is free of corruption? Is any firm or organization absolutely above board and honest. If so, they must be, as one accountant told me: 'On the verge of bankruptcy or so bloody wealthy they've forgotten all the fiddles.'

Apart from rumblings at local authority level in 1970, a Somerset farming company was fined £1,650 with £30,000 costs, and the managing director was sent to prison for two years, the company secretary being sentenced to nine months, after a 28-day hearing concerning the defrauding of the Ministry of Agriculture. The question of the payment of corn subsidies came out strongly during the trial, and one manager said that it was common knowledge that subsidies were being claimed from the Ministry on corn that never left the farm. Implicated in the case was a former secretary, described by a prosecution witness as one of the greatest forgers of this century.

If the economic climate produces fraud, so will events themselves. There was a considerable fuss about the police officers who were drafted to Wales for duty during the Investiture of Prince Charles in 1969. They found themselves so much out of pocket on their expenses that they filled in some blank bills to make up the difference between the allowable rate of £1 7*s* 6*d* and the £2 12*s* 6*d* which they had paid. Two female police officers were fined £75 each and two male officers £100 each.

The distinction between the abuse of position and outright fraud can become a misty area in which it is difficult to see the wood for the trees. For instance, one could make a case for conspiracy when, as happened, a bank manager had an arrangement with an insurance broker to push a certain type of fairly expensive policy on to a number of the more affluent customers of the bank. By tradition, you naturally trust your own bank manager who should be a man of the utmost probity and acumen. His persistent pushing of this particular policy aroused the suspicions of one customer, who happened to know a great deal about insurance. It was later found that the broker was paying the bank manager most handsomely for his services. Conspiracy is a crime committed when two or more persons combine together to execute some act for the purpose of injuring some other person or the public, and it is a misdemeanour at common law. When the manager was called to head office to account for his actions, he protested that he had not injured anybody to the best of his knowledge. In fact, it was a very good policy, otherwise he would not have recommended it. The bank solicitor quickly pointed out that conspiracy has implicit in its definition the fact that it can be regarded as existing if it involved the agreement of two or more people to do some unlawful act or to do some lawful act by unlawful means. The bank manager still tried to argue it out, but it was quite obvious that he had accepted a retainer from the insurance broker for pushing this particular policy. The upshot was that he resigned rather than wait to be fired or demoted, and he eventually went in with the broker as a partner, doing rather well for himself as a result.

It is not generally realized, in fact, that bank managers up till recently did have a direct financial interest in selling insurance policies to bank customers, and it was a poor manager who could not add £2,000 a year or more to his income by this means. A 1970 estimate suggested that 17 per cent of all life assurance in Britain was sold by bank managers. An average commission per sale would be upwards of £200. But most of the banks have now clamped down on a practice which was obviously open to abuse. They realized that the bank customer, like the patient in the doctor's surgery, is intensely vulnerable and entirely at the mercy of the traditionally respected 'professional man'.

Many conmen have recognized the value of the professional image, and the success of most frauds depends on the image. This applies even on the race course. Apart from the race itself, there is about the atmosphere of a meeting a constant suggestion that easy money is to be made. Besides, in the racing industry people are different. The chaps are more manly and free and easy, the gals always seem more attractive. Despite this aura, racing is an industry and, like other industries, it attracts its own hangers-on, and for the naïve and the innocent there is always a lurking belief that they might bring off a lucky bet and go home rich, and for this reason they snatch at any chance of rubbing shoulders with those who are said to be in the know. Although horse doping comes and goes, it is practically impossible to fix a race, and, despite the serious study of form by professional punters, it is sheer luck that wins many a race.

One of the most remarkable operators I ever met in the racing world was not a man but a woman of sixty, as spry as a horse flea with a taste for champagne cocktails and hired Daimlers. It would be quite inaccurate to portray her as golden-hearted and likeable when she was, candidly, hard, grasping and mean. She was one of the few professional con-women without some experience of prostitution in her youth, and for thirty years she used fraud only when she was in dire need of money. Most of the time she seemed to live with young men on the fringe of show business, because she was, despite her age, an attractive woman. Her most marked accomplishment was to egg suckers on and edge her way into circles where the big money circulated, and she was not above touching them for a loan, which she never repaid. As an exponent of parasitic survival in a hard world she was hard to beat.

For some years she teamed up with a man who was several years her junior, and there was in their first meeting at a cocktail party a touch of irony, because she was under the mistaken impression that he was an oil company executive. When it came down to it, he was a quick-buck racecourse operator who lived by his wits. Together, they represented the ideal combination for a plan which she devised and which they still use from time to time. The plan itself has one drawback in that it has to be financed in advance, because they book in at a hotel in Newmarket or one of the other centres before the racing season starts, passing themselves off as being connected with the stables. They then strike up an acquaintance with any man who looks fairly affluent and they treat him not too ostentatiously to dinner and drinks on a number of occasions. In the course of conversation the 'husband' laughingly admits that his 'wife' has the golden touch in business. He has never known her fail yet. This seed is left to grow in the sucker's mind. Then an outing is arranged, and she further butters up the sucker who is, by this time, fascinated by her astuteness. The racing season has by this time started. He invites the couple to dinner and they become even better acquainted. Soon the 'husband' happens to mention his wife's system for making what he refers to as pin money. She laughingly asserts that £1,000 a month is hardly pin money to some people. The sucker is staggered but tries to conceal his astonishment. £1,000 a month! In the end he can hardly contain himself and he diffidently asks how on earth she manages it. She hesitates at first, but finally admits that it has to do with the gee-gees. Racing has been her hobby for years, but she has made it a rule never to go mad with her betting. In fact, she considers betting a mug's game. You only have to look at the bookies to know that. But . . . yes, she does have her own little system, it is true, and she has been using it for twenty years without a single failure.

The sucker is now ready for it. It takes very little to persuade him that as he has been so awfully kind to them, so . . . well, there is a horse called Absalom's Joy and she proposes backing it at twelve to one. Now, if he would like to come in on it, he will find that it will become the favourite. Anybody with an elementary knowledge of racing can pick a favourite in advance. The odds will come down to four to one. When this happens they will lay off a proportion of the bets.

This looks very much like inside information, but it is far from it, because the preliminary shuffle is a ritual and the odds can be estimated by a simpleton. Still bedazzled by her know-how, especially in view of the fact that he knows practically nothing about racing, the sucker says he will put £25 on it. She is vastly amused. £25 is nothing. He must remember that she intends laying off her bets—that is, she will also be betting *against* the horse—so it will pay him to put a packet on. She herself will be making a stake of £2,000. He hurriedly rakes up his own £2,000 and his cheque is cleared after she puts it through her own account. Any bank will clear a cheque at once if you pay for the telephone call. She then explains that this is a complete certainty because if Absalom's Joy wins they will be £48,000 to the good, but by laying off the bets, they will still stand to gain £10,000. Either way, they cannot go wrong.

Of course, she has not even placed the bet. All the talked of hedged bets is merely a smokescreen. If the favourite does win, she tells him, she will just go to the bookie and collect and then they can share it out. She vanishes into the crowd and is never seen again. By the time the sucker starts to look for her and her husband, they are on their way back to London. On the other hand, if the favourite does not win, she gives him a rubber cheque, immediately closes her bank account, changes her name and starts all over again. It does not matter which way it goes, she stands to escape with his money.

Why are people so gullible? By some mysterious process, greed overcomes caution. The very suspicious appearance of a 'good thing' should put people on their guard, but it doesn't, because so few people expect to be done. Even today, with rapid communication in the press, radio and television, some staggering frauds are coolly perpetrated time after time. It seems that despite the activities of many consumer organizations and other public watchdogs, it is actually easier to perpetrate a fraud than at any other time. Practically every week the newspapers contain details of new unit trusts and share co-operatives, and while all of these pass through the sieve of the advertisement department so that only the most reputable are accepted for publication, a certain number manage to publicize themselves in other ways. Even where apparently reputable ones are concerned, there have in recent years been some spectacular crashes from which the directors have emerged quite unscathed.

Three brothers using the name of Mandeville used to be very active in this game, and the guiding light was Alexis, a charming fellow who was always good for a drink. He had been in business ever since Mandeville senior, now deceased, drummed into him that you could not beat business for making money. He spent his formative years in the office of a stockbroker but then broke away to establish a firm called the London and Paris Exchange Limited, which would introduce buyers and sellers of shares, eliminating the stockbroker and his expensive commission. The

Exchange would make a small profit on the buying and selling price.

Alexis Mandeville was probably a genius, because there was about the plan something so simple and elementary that even a hostile stockbroking fraternity could not see anything wrong with it. The most hardened business man might be forgiven for thinking that the London and Paris Exchange Limited was a veritable godsend. The sprouting of the firm was rapid, and the three Mandeville brothers somehow got together enough money to acquire large offices in London and Paris and to give employment to several hundred people. The clients were meanwhile in receipt of daily information sheets which told them which shares to buy. It was an unusual morning when the mail failed to yield several thousand pounds in cheques, postal orders and cash. The investors were pleased to find that when the Exchange guaranteed a profit, that profit was promptly paid. Confidence built up quickly in London and Paris, and people who had financed some of the 'special' share-buying operations of the Exchange were thrilled to receive cheques for £10 to £25 as their profit on an investment of, say, £100, which sum remained in what the Mandevilles called the Exchange Pool to finance other buyings. The legend of the Mandeville brothers and their astuteness grew and grew until people in their thousands were clamouring to let the London and Paris Exchange Limited handle their money. In one somewhat unpleasant episode, when a blackmail attempt was made, Alexis had the criminals charged and they were sent to prison for a year. In the meantime the Mandeville empire went from strength to strength. They even bought an existing magazine under cover of another company and used the City pages to promote the London and Paris Exchange Limited in the guise of advice to investors.

The brothers themselves lived the life of Reilly, paying themselves high salaries and expenses. They were all generous men, donating regularly to charities, financing the schemes of others and not seeming to care whether they saw their money back or not.

Then, without any warning, there was a heavy run on withdrawals which the firm could not meet, and that was the end of the London and Paris Exchange Limited. Liabilities £424,437. Assets £3. They had, as the saying goes in the city, been living on their own tail, paying profits out of assets.

But it was not the end of the Mandevilles by any means,

because within a few months they started the Financial Mail Operating Trust, which ran a number of what they called 'blind pools'. In construction they were similar to unit trusts. Once more the advertisements appeared and small investors were invited to put certain sums of money into investment pools relating to a number of expanding industries with a guaranteed dividend of 30 per cent. Although the Mandevilles were now known to be questionable figures in the world of finance, the public nevertheless responded, and it was once again the same old story with the brothers going through the morning mail to see how much had been presented to them by a gullible public. Side by side with the blind pools idea was another scheme whereby investors could pay for selected shares by instalments, the proviso being that they would own the shares only after the full sum had been paid up. A surprising number of clients stopped paying after a few instalments, but others, who did pay up completely were unable to obtain acceptance certificates from the Mandevilles. The explanation was simple enough. The Mandevilles never bought the shares on behalf of their clients. When doomsday dawned, it took three years to try and reckon up how much money they had taken, a tentative figure being £494,000, but it was probably more than twice that figure. They said they had only £55 left out of the latest venture. After thirty years of fraud and swindling, in which time they handled untold wealth, they were sent to prison for six years apiece. A few weeks after their release one of them committed suicide. The other two vanished.

Chapter Five

The International Fraud Cartels

In the course of my work I went to West Berlin, which is not unlike Tel Aviv in many ways, often gaudy and razzamataz, full of mainchance operators engaged in anything from wholesale drug peddling to the traffic in girls which used to be called, rather quaintly, the white slave trade. In such a city you can become an overnight millionaire, you can be seduced, ravished, robbed, corrupted, murdered and encased in concrete, all in a matter of a few hours. Altogether, an interesting, occasionally horrifying and a very expensive city where a woman can cost more than a meal in a first-class restaurant. Comparatively few people go as tourists to West Berlin, because it offers few diversions for the Everyman family, and you will always see far more men than women on the streets, most of them wearing beautifully cut suits and carrying briefcases. As you approach Checkpoint Charlie which is near the East-West frontier, the people grow less and you see a Harry Lime on every street corner. But down on what used to be the Kurfurstendam there is at attempt at gay commercialism and free enterprise, and the stores are very colourful. Behind this layer of sell-sell-sell the thick layer of grey concrete offices starts, and there are workrooms, coffee shops, bars and the wholesale warehouses. And behind that are the quieter areas with more offices, apparently reputable and lending substance to the finance belt, which is sprinkled with brokerage houses and a few doctors and dentists.

The man I wanted to see was English, one of the remnants of World War Two, who had lived in places as far apart as Sicily, Rome, Birmingham, London, Paris, Stockton-on-Tees, and now Berlin. He served in the Tank Corps in the war, was in the Western Desert, where he was lightly injured at Derna and then discharged in the undistinguished rank of junior NCO.

Quite early in life he had discovered a talent for planning, but at the same time he had sufficient insight to acknowledge an inability to get on with other people on a face to face basis. He wrote a convincing letter but in discussion he was hopeless, and what he considered to be a character deficiency caused many inner battles. He tried to cure it, but he just could not manage it, and for some years after the war he wandered from country to country, doing odd jobs, meeting equally odd people, whom he seemed to attract, and making a little money here and there. During this period he did not care what happened to him, but he was still secretly anxious to create a definite pattern in his life. Somewhere along the line he met a Swedish woman who recognized his potential and introduced him to her husband, from whom she was parted though still in a business partnership. Their speciality was foreign real estate in which they had a minute interest with other business people, but they were now branching out on their own and had opened offices in the main centres of Europe to cash in on the building boom. What they really needed was a co-ordinator and the now middle-aged Englishman without any attachments seemed to be the man for the job. So here he was in Berlin without any regrets except that the city was not his idea of heaven, although he had a pleasant apartment and an understanding girl friend.

It is possible to draw a 'family tree' for many businesses, showing which branch does what, but the small empire which he now headed was not like that. It was often a self-defeating growth, the branches being grown for a particular purpose and then lopped off.

'So how are things?' I asked.

'Changed,' he admitted. 'Property is—' He made a thumbs down gesture. 'You have to be flexible these days.'

We talked about the Desert War for a time—he had recently been back to Derna and Tobruk, Mersa Matruh, which had been the butt of music hall comics, and to Cairo—and then we went out to lunch. We went back to the office and he ushered me through his place of work into another room where three elderly men sprang up from their desks and were introduced. 'They've all got prison records. Two of them were in the SS, but they've done their time, so let's forget it. It's quite tough for ex-Nazis in Berlin, nobody will give them a job if they have a record. That's how I got hold of these.'

'What about the third man?' I asked.

He smiled briefly. In Berlin to talk about a third man has some significance. 'He worked in one of the camps. But come and have a look . . .'

The charts on the walls showed the current situation throughout Europe, and I was particularly interested to see one labelled Manchester. He said that it was a kind of pilot project, because Manchester was considered one of the best British cities for that kind of thing.

'We break down the population into income groups and study it from a sociological point of view, and then we tailor the scheme accordingly.' He opened a filing cabinet and produced a weighty folder. 'Now, Manchester—yes, just look at this breakdown of professions. It lists everything.'

'But who does all this groundwork?' I asked.

'Part of it we pay for. Social survey firms will supply this kind of data, but some of it is done by our own people. One of the things we have been doing is hiring university graduates for short periods to run social surveys. Cheap labour, very enthusiastic, and they don't know the purpose of the survey. It isn't their concern, anyway.'

Regardless of the location of the operation, the pattern is always similar. As soon as a survey is completed, another organization is set up to sell securities or shares or insurance, and profits and premiums which exceed those of the more respectable and old-established companies are offered as a come-on. Not all companies which offer high profits to customers are necessarily crooked, of course.

The Berlin organization is extraordinarily thorough. They do not stop at selling faulty insurance and other schemes to the business sector, which is among the most vulnerable, they also sell to students, to single women, to parents who believe that they are hallmarking money for the education of their children. One scheme was aimed at middle-management in industry, another at shop workers. The actual methods of selling insurance and assurance on the basis of the firm 'feeding on its own tail' and paying claims out of income has been described elsewhere.

But can this be called a cartel in fraud? A cartel is properly defined as 'a manufacturers' union to control production, marketing, arrangements, prices, etc.'. In view of the fact that this concern not only originates but also markets and pockets the profits, it certainly does seem to qualify for the term. For all its widespread operation throughout Europe, it consists of only three people topped by an elaborate superstructure consisting in the main of phony insurance schemes which do not pay off.

I had the opportunity of examining one period of six months, in which time companies were started in Britain, France and Italy, each of them being keyed to national conditions. Some of the schemes offered payment by instalments, others required moderate premiums, and others had a built-in inducement with a kind of lottery for cars, cheap holidays abroad, kitchenware and so on. There was no fraud element in the gifts. They were given out and some clients did rather well for themselves out of it. The aim was, of course, to create a credible bait for the future. The total number of companies started was 36, and during the first six months an average of £500 to £1,000 a week was taken by each company. Before the end of the first six months well over £1 million was in the coffers, and the organization was beginning to 'feed on its tail', paying claims out of capital, which was on deposit at a Zurich bank.

The English director now had a meeting with his Swedish employers and the figures were carefully scrutinized. There is about this kind of operation a 'close-down' figure, and it is governed by the amount of erosion of capital by the pay-out figures. Exactly when the operation is closed down is entirely up to the operator, and in this case the takings had fallen drastically to as little as £250 a week by each company. The Swedes decided to call a halt. In a matter of hours all the companies had vanished. In some cases the offices full of promotion brochures and empty filing cabinets were discovered by angry clients. The police arrived and, some weeks later, the matter was placed in the hands of Interpol. But . . . there was no real trace. The network was baffling and it was almost impossible to discover who was behind it. What actually happened was that the contents of the offices were loaded on to hired vans overnight to be stored in anonymous packing cases in repositories to remain there for an indefinite period, the fees being paid regularly by banker's order from a holding account in each country.

In recent years the crashes of supposedly large insurance companies in Britain have been well publicized, but still the public falls for it time after time. Provided one multiplies sufficiently over a large area like the Continent, it is easy to avoid revealing publicity. In Britain the investigation falls first to the police but later to the Department of Trade. An investigator told me that while business could be started in Britain by the simple device of filling in an official form and paying a shilling or two stamp duty for registration, this type of fraud was bound to continue. Despite the warnings issued by the professional underwriting associations, wildcat insurance schemes go on being promoted and the public falls for it, so that when a crash does occur the bona fide insurance companies are called in to pick up the pieces and provide cover for the defrauded customers. As for the culprits, it is rare for them to be identified let alone apprehended, especially when a cut-out system is used.

If insurance is an easy way of making money, art forgery must run a close second. Art forgery is not, as many people seem to think, necessarily the forgery of well-known paintings, sculpture and objets d'art but the fabrication of work which might be attributed to certain artists. This is because the whereabouts of all famous works of art is more or less known to museums and individual collectors and the legion of art historians and university authorities. For instance, one would not dream of forging the Mona Lisa because we all know that the one in the Louvre is the genuine one (or is it?). Even van Meegeren, painter, art dealer and forger of Keizersgracht 321, Amsterdam, whose faked Vermeers fooled Goering, did not produce copies of known pictures but canvases which might be taken for Vermeers, including the famous *The Woman Taken in Adultery*. There is in this a fine point of law, and while it may vary between countries, it should be kept in mind that the enthusiastic and often rather greedy collector prefers to pick up a painting which the seller thinks 'may be' by a particular master. This is very much the collector's look-out. The outstanding example of this factor at work involved the work of Alceo Dossena, probably the greatest imitative sculptor of all time and noted nowadays for a life-size *Annunciation*, done in wood after the painting by Simone Martini (1283–1344). The work itself was superb, but Dossena unfortunately stuck old pieces of wood together with a modern glue, and this was his undoing.

It is impossible to praise Dossena's work too highly. From 1916 until the thirties he was without doubt the world's greatest forger-sculptor and, like many other creative men, he was supremely unconscious of the fact that his talents were being used to put money into the pockets of his 'backers'. Very few creative forgers, whether in painting, sculpture or other forms, are the vendors of their own work. There are people in between, and they are the ones who make the real money, while the artist is generally badly rewarded. This is the way of the world, and I have elementary personal proof of it. I happen to have a modest talent for woodcarving, my speciality being the primitive figures of many different cultures. They look absolutely authentic, so much so that on one occasion a rather weird but affluent individual sidled up to me at an exhibition of my work and suggested that we could together do very well for ourselves if I produced my primitives which he would place on the American collector market. Sensing that here was something which might please Mr Evans, my bank manager, I asked how much he had in mind. He offered an average of £20 per sculpture. This was quite attractive, because I can as a rule produce a fair-sized carving in about eight hours. Then as an afterthought I asked him how much he intended charging his American clients. He was quite frank when he said that he would charge about £60 minimum and probably a lot more. My minimum £20 per piece was, of course, guaranteed, and there was no risk. This was a good example of how the art forgery business is conducted. I might add that I still carve for my own amusement.

Alceo Dossena was a simple stone-mason, and when on leave from the Poggi Mirteto on Christmas Eve, 1916, he brought with him a Madonna carved in relief, which he wanted to sell to buy presents. While taking a drink in a wine shop in the via Mario de Fiori, Rome, he showed the carving to the landlord, who did not wish to buy it, but he called in a man called Alfredo Fasoli, a goldsmith, who was struck by its beauty. Dossena did not admit that he himself had carved it, but explained that he was selling it for a friend. Fasoli paid one hundred lire for the Madonna and, when he got back to his workshop, he examined it under a magnifying glass to find that it was not as old as he had imagined. It was simply a replica and a very convincing one. He sat up half the night, looking at the fine detail and marvelling that Italy still had carvers capable of doing such work. And then he started looking beyond the Madonna into the kingdom of gold. Next day he started searching for the peasant soldier, Dossena, and by a miracle he found him. He asked for the name of the craftsman who had made the Madonna, and Dossena finally said that he had made it. He thought that Fasoli might want his money back, and he had already bought presents for his family. Fasoli smiled at him. They must have a drink together. Over the wine the goldsmith suggested a partnership and suggested that Dossena should keep quiet about it.

Only a few months later Dossena was discharged from the Italian army and arrived on Fasoli's doorstep, scarcely believing that the agreement would be honoured. But it was, and Fasoli set him up in a workshop, suggesting that he first carve a medieval figure. To his amazement, the figure was carved rapidly and before his eyes, without any drawings or a model. Dossena said that he had never had any lessons but carved by instinct. Fasoli wrapped up the figure and rushed off, and he was absent for several hours. He sold the figure for 3,000 lire and rewarded Dossena with 200 lire.

It should be understood that other art forgers were operating in Rome at that time, but their work was often stiff and lacking the flowing grace of the true medieval style. Under Dossena's chisels it was as though a medieval craftsman was at work. Fasoli tried to keep it to himself, but the news did leak out to a small circle of middlemen, who crowded into the workshop to watch the master at work. It was inevitable that some of them nobbled Dossena, much to the rage and chagrin of Fasoli. He could do very little to control his prodigy, who protested that he needed money. Sometimes there were seven or more figures being carved at the same time on the bench, and it was unbelievable that the quality could be maintained, but it was, and in due course experienced valuers, museum curators and cultured collectors were all taken in. Fasoli meantime organized another side of the business, the forgery of certificates of authenticity.

Dossena was dazed and stupefied by the amount of money he was making. The pockets of his working smock were stuffed full of bank notes, but he had no time to spend it. In the end he declared that he must have some time off to enjoy himself. He was married and he had children, but his wife was completely uninterested in his work, although she loved his money. It was her attitude that drove him to the brothels and the wine shops, and for a time he was courted by the middlemen, who had done so well out of his work. Even at this stage he did not realize fully that his work was being passed off as genuine antique, although he had sculpted in styles from the Roman to the Ancient Greek.

He had spent vast sums of money on fun and good living when an order arrived for a full-sized Renaissance tomb after Mino da Fiesole with an inscription referring to the Savelli family on the stonework. Size meant nothing to Dossena. After making some rough sketches, he selected his stone and then went straight into the realization of what was to be known in future years, and is still known, as the Tomb of Savelli. It has been described as a masterpiece of High Gothic, and it was created by a man who never had an art lesson in his life. The fee paid to him was 25,000 lire. The Savelli Tomb was sold over and over again, reaching a peak price of six million lire. With it went a set of cleverly forged documents, including a receipt in the hand of the master stonemason, Mino da Fiesole himself.

Dossena was about to resume his day-to-day work on medieval figurines for Fasoli and others when an order arrived for an Athene. It was to be about 5 feet 6 inches tall, and he completed it in a matter of weeks. When finished it rivalled the finest art of Ancient Greece. Many learned papers were written by authorities on the 'find', and it was said to be the best example of the sculpture of the period. They were in for a shock when Dossena finally woke up to reality after discovering that he, the creator, was the worst paid. It was only the stringent need for money to pay for his wife's funeral that created a situation in which he found himself temporarily penniless. He tried to raise loans from the dealers who had once begged him to create pieces of sculpture for them. Furious and angered by their refusal, he went to a lawyer and issued a damning statement to the effect that he, Dossena, had created the Tomb of Savelli, the Athene and hundreds of small figures in stone and wood, but in no single case had he passed them off as genuine antiques.

The art world scoffed, tried to laugh it off, and looked the other way until he started naming names and giving dates. This was enough to cast doubt on the clan of art dealers, including Jacob Hirsch, a wealthy Paris dealer, who was aggravated beyond measure, because he happened to be the man who handled the Tomb of Savelli and was able to increase the price. The Athene had also been through his gallery, and he had sold it for six million lire. He declared that he would put an end to all this nonsense by confronting this stupid illiterate ape Dossena in Rome.

Many dealers and authorities were present at Dossena's studio when Hirsch strolled in. Most of them had examined the Athene at close quarters and they knew every scratch and chisel mark. Hirsch was incredibly rude to Dossena, who listened to the threats and tried to reply. It is possible in retrospect to be kind to Hirsch and believe that he did not know that the Athene was a forgery at the time when he sold it. Alternatively, he may have suspected that it was a forgery, but as it had passed through so many learned hands he may have disbelieved his own forebodings. Whatever the answer might be, he was quite determined to show Dossena up and silence the ugly rumours which were now discrediting the entire art dealing world.

Unable to reply, Dossena finally went to the heap of rubble at the back of the studio and from it pulled out the stone fingers of the Athene, which he presented to a thunderstruck Hirsch with the invitation to fit them to the hand of the sculpture. When the figure was finished his client had instructed him to make it more authentic by chipping off a few bits and pieces. Without another word, Hirsch stalked out of the studio, already trying to formulate a campaign to save his face. During the next year or two there were many rows and controversies. No sooner did some authority or other assert the authenticity of a piece than Dossena proved beyond doubt that it had come from his chisel. Angry collectors sued dealers and dealers sued experts. The Berlin Museum of Antiquities was drawn into it when it was alleged that the Greek sculpture, Goddess Enthroned, was neither Greek nor ancient. Dossena confirmed that it was one of his works.

The fascination of Dossena is that every single piece which came from his studio on the banks of the Tiber was an original and not a copy of any known work, and even the famous Tomb of Savelli, which really started it all and now rests in the Boston Museum of Fine Arts, is entirely original. As Boston paid 100,000 dollars for it, they are naturally loath to label it a Dossena forgery and put it in the vaults, where it will not be seen. Boston is not alone in giving space to the works of Dossena. Cleveland has Pisano's Madonna and Child, while in New York the Metropolitan Museum has on show a Greek goddess. Only when pressed will these and other museums admit that they are forgeries. Dossena, who died a pauper in 1937, after a series of law suits which benefited him not at all, would have viewed his continuing fame with wry amusement. He might also be aggravated to know that his work is now valued at between one and two million dollars.

Although Dossena happens once in a lifetime, it should not be thought that this type of art forgery is infrequent, because there are many parts of Italy where you can pick up a medieval Madonna made only last week. The Italians have a particular aptitude for producing sculpture and other works of art in any style at will. As in the days of Dossena, however, the rapacious middleman is still active, but one can hardly blame the craftsmen themselves. For instance, my good friend, Gino Masero, is the leading master carver in Britain, and he works in the grand style of the Baroque, but he can also produce in the Grinling Gibbons manner and, indeed, did so when he helped to restore Gibbons rich carvings in the Old Admiralty Board-room in London. Equally, he can carve panels which are more Aztec than Aztec. Yet even this fine craftsman will not mind me saying that he often has to wait for commissions for long periods at a time. If this applies to a man who is carver to the College of Arms and whose work is highly prized by collectors, then consider the lesser craftsman who is approached by unscrupulous dealers.

Nowadays the organization of art fraud is centred mainly in Belgium, although the artists and craftsmen are located throughout Europe. A certain percentage of the replicas produced are, frankly, below standard and they take in only the naïve tourist and amateur collector who is still groping his way towards an understanding of his particular field. If we exempt the junk, then something like 25 per cent can be put in the quality category, and it includes exact replicas of jewellery from different periods. This is not unusual. It has been going on for some years, and a London middleman told me that he handles several thousand pounds' worth of it every year. 'I am not concerned with what antique dealers do with this reproduction jewellery, but I do happen to know that a lot of them mix it up with the genuine stuff on their display trays. I charge one price for it, and what they charge is up to them, but they expect to make up to 500 per cent profit. It depends on their class of customer. Let's keep the record straight, though, and say that this reproduction stuff is gold or pinchbeck and the stones are genuine. If they are buffed up on a wheel and scratched a bit, that gives them a worn look, makes them more attractive.'

This is, of course, the cheap end of art forgery, but it is nevertheless highly organized with workshops in Paris staffed by elderly jewellers who cannot get jobs elsewhere in a relatively small industry. The craftsmen work from detailed drawings which are generally prepared by art students anxious to earn a pound or two by working from exhibits in collections throughout the country, including the Victoria and Albert Museum, London, which also offers the free use of the National Art Library with more than 300,000 books, pamphlets and periodicals. Photographs are not much use to the manufacturing jeweller except for general reference purposes and colour matching. What he prefers is a detailed pen and ink drawing, showing the methods of stone setting, the way clasps were fashioned and the nature of the metals used.

In terms of industrial structure the Belgium HQ organization is not large, because it depends mainly on experts scattered throughout Europe. One is German, who is *persona non grata* in his own country, and his speciality is medieval art. He is not himself an artist but could be called a self-taught art historian, because he has for many years pursued the subject with national thoroughness and tenacity. He now has a collection of several thousand books and prints and a card index which enables him to produce reference material in a matter of moments. Trained in pre-war Germany as an engineer, he served in the Wermacht for several years, went into the postwar black market when he could not find a job, and finally fled to France and then on to Belgium. In this period he visited galleries and read everything worth reading about medieval art. As a man he is perfectly likeable and he is quite open about his business. He is perpetually amused by the cupidity of collectors, but at no time has he ever attempted to label one of the manufactured masterpieces as being from the brush of a definite artist. What happens is this: an intermediary or a shady dealer located somewhere in Europe notifies an interest in a certain type of canvas or panel which might be attributed to a certain period. The name of an artist might, or might not, be mentioned. What is mentioned is a tentative price, and then some haggling or horse trading takes place, ending as a rule on an amicable note. It is not practice to pass over any cash at this point. A recent order was for a triptych 'in the Cologne style'. The German located a few colour transparencies of genuine pieces in national collections throughout the world, and travelled to Rotterdam, where he spent a week with an artist who happened to have a gift for producing such work. He and the German met after the war, when the Dutchman claimed to paint by supernatural aid. His financial affairs were chaotic, but he had thrown up a good job in order to pursue his interest in painting. There was no market for his work. The German offered to remedy all that. He would pay off the debts and guarantee a small retainer with bonuses. It entailed painting up to twenty pieces a year and by this means he was able to continue with his own development as an artist. He never asked any questions about the little masterpieces, because he was too busy finding wood old enough on which to paint, but even this was overcome in time. One of the most important aspects of this type of reproduction was that a built-in imperfection was expected, and he also spent a lot of time weathering the work. For two years he painted nothing but fragments of masterpieces, and they were floated on to the tourist market in Rome, Siena and Pisa with a standard legend that they had been looted in the war and hidden away. The game was up when a buyer who knew no better tried to smuggle his purchase through London Airport and a Customs officer with an interest in art gravely advised him that it was quite unnecessary in view of the fact that the painting was probably a replica and modern.

Paintings are surprisingly simple to copy, but the drawback is that the big-money market for such forgeries is very small. There is without doubt some truth in the legend of the wealthy collector who buys stolen pictures only to hang them in rooms or vaults to which only he has access. Such a man is naturally vulnerable and a target for fakers. Since the Impressionists started commanding such high prices as an investment a number of quite passable fakes of this genre have come to light. Elmyr de Hory, the talented son of Translyvanian parents, spent an uncomfortable time in a German refugee camp. When peace broke out he went, penniless, to Paris and almost by a sheer fluke discovered that he could draw and paint in the style of Modigliani, Picasso and other contemporaries. He sold his first attempt, a Picasso sketch, without any trouble and he made enough money to buy a villa on the Ibiza. From this base he flooded the market through intermediaries with more than one thousand gouaches, water colours and sketches to a paper value of sixty million dollars. The final scandal blew up in 1967, and his two confederates went to prison. He was deported from France to Ibiza, where he still lives. In fact, line drawings in the Picasso manner are relatively simple to fabricate, and there is in London a forger who uses an epidiascope to simply project the illustrations from books on Piccaso on to a drawing block. Nothing could be simpler, and sketches of this sort are sold to American tourists at high prices. The legal position is rather odd, because it is doubtful whether any prosecution would succeed on the basis of plain forgery or 'passing off', because the seller always refrains from saying plainly that this is a Picasso or a Matisse, and in reply to a direct question he will generally reply: 'It seems to be, but I wouldn't know, not for sure.' In the psychology of such a transaction, the buyer is sure that he has got himself a fantastic bargain, and so he finally plunges in and pays up. I once did so and bought a small Utrillo; it was years before I realized that the original was in Paris, on show to the public. Obviously, there is no redress, even if you can trace the person who sold you the picture. This was discovered in 1938 by Lucien Pissarro. A painting said to be from the brush of his father and bearing what he alleged to be his father's forged signature was being offered for sale in London. His application for an injunction to have the signature deleted was turned down, and the painting was finally sold at a handsome figure as a genuine Pissarro.

Very few legal actions involving art forgeries attract more than passing attention and a few days' publicity. For instance, few people will recall that in 1959 a Gothic carving, Madonna with a Bunch of Grapes, was hurriedly withdrawn from the Dorotheum, Austria's famous saleroom. It turned out to be from the studio of Joseph Rifesser, a carver who still lives in the South Tyrol. Like Dossena before him, he was not aware that his work in the style of 1380 was being passed off, and he received only £30 for the piece which eventually appeared at the Dorotheum.

The first intimation that one or more major gangs of art forgers were at work in Europe was demonstrated with certainty in 1962 when the London art dealer, Jacques O'Hana, a friend of Picasso, was instrumental in helping with investigations which led to the arrest of the talented 32-year-old Paris artist, Jean-Pierre Schecroun, who was described by the French police as a 'virtuoso of art forgery', quite capable of producing a water colour, sketch or pastel by Picasso or Miro within an hour. His other specialities were Chagall and Léger, and profits of more than £70,000 were netted from two pictures within a year. The ring, which operated in Britain, Switzerland and Germany, did not merely produce the pictures but also provided forged certificates of authenticity with the imprint of famous Paris galleries. Two paintings by Braque and Miro were offered to Jacques O'Hana, who thought it odd that two young Frenchmen should be in possession of such famous pictures. At the time he said that the pictures were faked but they were the best fakes he had ever seen.

At best, art forgery is restricted by the size of the market, and other possibilities abound. But as coiners forge money, the art fabricators produce a means of making money. The Belgium consortium which I mentioned earlier employs forty painters, sculptors, makers of icons and various other pieces, and they sell in a wide range of prices, from £20 to £5,000 or even more. The level of artistic accomplishment is high and it is backed by an intimate knowledge of the technicalities to produce the antique effect. One of the best of them is Francisco, a Basque of nearly half a century's experience of all forms of painting. He was drawn into the syndicate in the first place when he was found painting reproduction icons in Paris and selling them as reproductions. He was at that time debilitated and dispirited, he drank a great deal, and his rehabilitation took a full year, after which he was paid a regular salary to produce one small painting every month in the style of Corot. At that time there was a terrific demand for Corot. He steeped himself in the style of the master and his work successfully fooled even the most knowledgeable dealers and collectors. In time, however, he became very interested in the chemistry of art, the composition of paint, pigment and canvas, and he is now the 'technical director' of the group. As he explained to me, to get hold of the facts of, say, Byzantine painting, one should read Cennini's report on the methods used by Giotto. Down the ages artists have used many different kinds of pigment, lye and tempera, and varnishes alone represent a lifetime of study. Francisco produced a rare book to illustrate a point. It was the Lucca Manuscript, one of the most sought after of all formulary. A copy can fetch as much as £1,000—or did, because an enterprising entrepeneur recently began to provide photo-copies at £100 each. But Francisco does not rely entirely on the Lucca Manuscript. He also has a copy of the Hermeneia of Dionysus of 1350, the Mappae Claviculae of the thirteenth century and the book of Heraclius of the eighth century. Together, they represent an exceptionally fine forgers' library. In the unlikely event of a copy of all of them reaching a saleroom at the same time, it is unlikely that they could be bought for less than £3,500 to £5,000. Francisco, who would not part with them for a fortune, was at pains to point out that if one is creating an authentic period painting, the work must approximate to the conditions in which the original was painted. At that moment a large canvas was being created, and the conditions resembled those of a laboratory rather than a studio. Egg yolk was being mixed with fig juice. The figs had been bought by a 'courier' in Rome and rushed to Belgium by air. The juice was of a certain colour, and, as far as using the yolk of battery eggs was concerned, this was naturally unthinkable. Only free range eggs would give the right yolk consistency. Pigments and egg yolk should not be blended with an electric mixer but rubbed through a silk sieve. And so on. One could compile a *vade mecum* on the methods of yesterday for the use of today's forgers, but wide gaps would be bound to occur. Canvas, for instance, is machine woven nowadays, and so it is necessary to boil it for hours on end and then lay it out in the hot sun and splash it with sodium hydrate, which leaves great brown marks. It is this kind of discoloration which imparts what can only be described as a patina-like show-through when the pigments are laid on it. When the painting is finished, it must be aged. Van Meegeren used to bake his masterpieces, but technical advances have been made since he died of a broken heart. Experiments with infra-red 'cookery' produced passable results, but the real secret, according to Francisco, is in the varnishing. The varnish must be rubbed on by hand, not smoothly brushed in a film. If the tempera is right and the exact thickness of the varnish is right, and the surface is heated to a precise temperature, the typical egg-shell cracking effect will be produced. At Francisco's request I have omitted one vital ingredient.

It was explained to me that while the greatest care is taken to fabricate these pictures to methods as close to the original as possible, one could not, of course, hope to make them pass a full chemical analysis or the radiographic examination technique. Some of the pictures serve a variety of uses, especially when they are in the £25,000 range . . .

Let us suppose that Mr USA likes to be mistaken for a collector. He does have a small collection of pictures back home, all of them good but minor works. His annual visits to Europe figure in the Social Register when he and his wife do the galleries and many of the galleries do him. He was for many years an industrial kingpin. As far as knowing art is concerned, he knows what he likes, as the saying goes, and once he has taken a liking to a picture nothing will hold him back. His arrival in Paris is the signal to the dealers that the big spender is in town. Old canvasses are taken out and dusted down.

Sacha, one of the organizers of the consortium, lit his pipe. 'We would study this man. We would study everything about him, because he is a fanatic with his collecting. He is perhaps artistically blind, because his background is materialistic. One of our bright young gentlemen might arrange a short meeting at a gallery or a concert or some function of that kind. Or there is always the soirée. You know, the social life of Paris is the same as it always was. It is easy to get to know somebody through such circles. The purpose is simple, we want to make an assessment, to know what kind of man he is. Our young man majored in psychology, and so we can anticipate a most accurate assessment. We then leave it at that. For the next part we examine our stock. We have maybe thirty good ones ready. One of them is a minor Rembrandt, or it looks like a Rembrandt, if you understand. There are very few collectors who can resist a Rembrandt, it is the universal magnet. So we say yes, we will use the Rembrandt. Next, we arrange for some publicity so that the American gentleman will know about the existence of the Rembrandt. We have several associates who will do this for us, and one of them has an elegant apartment in a fashionable quarter. Let me say he is already an art collector but a minor one and he is quite well respected. He works for us now and then. It amuses him and, of course, the fee pleases him. So, one day we provide him with the Rembrandt and he grants it a place on the walls of his salon, but not too obviously. He then holds a social evening, a delightful cocktail party, something which the American attends. It is not difficult to make sure that he will come. He wishes to be in the swim, as they say. The social occasion is very tasteful. He accepts. There are not too many guests, but they are all people from our organization, no outsiders at all. They are introduced to the American, and he believes that they are all distinguished. A surgeon. An art expert. A composer. Perhaps a dozen or so. Of course, they are all poseurs, they are not real, but they are excellent actors, almost to the standard of the Comedie Française. One can respect them for that. The American is not very much at ease in their company. He is used to being the big man, but these are not the kind of people he would meet in the usual way. So he is maybe a little quiet. The champagne is good, everything is good. Soon his host shows off his pictures in two other rooms. Nobody else is present. Now, here is an interesting point. I show you eleven genuine paintings and one forgery and you will not detect the forgery if it is a good one, even if you are an expert. The mind is lulled by so much excellence. Even Picasso himself has acknowledged forgeries of his own style in gallery exhibitions. The master himself is deceived. Look at the Manet exhibition in London in 1944—so many fakes and forgeries. In 1958 Cazals, the famous French collector, gave £11,000 for a Fragonard. Very reasonable for a real Fragonard, not so cheap for a clever copy. This was a copy, so even the great Etienne Cazals was deceived. And recall Rudi Conventz in 1958 with all his Titians, Rembrandts, Cranachs—all fakes, many very poor, but all authenticated by Professor Kahns, the Professor of Art History at Halle. Of course, Kahns was half blind and Conventz was a fruit salesman.

'So the American looks at the good pictures. Everything is of the finest quality. He is dazzled. When you are a collector, there is always one more or one more you would like to possess. It is not always the excellence of the work, sometimes it is the legend or the story of the painting. It is an aura. The American is as covetous as any collector, he barely hides it. So by the time they reach the Rembrandt, he is in the right frame of mind. Of course, it is a fine Rembrandt but a small one and it is very attractive and perhaps not very well known, as his host points out.

'There the matter rests. The American perhaps returns to America, but it does not matter where the next act is staged. Before anything else, though, it is arranged that the Rembrandt shall be "stolen". A robbery is arranged and the report appears in the newspapers. It is the report we want, simply good honest publicity.

'One of our people now goes to the American. It is improbable that he knows about the Rembrandt being stolen. The picture is offered to him. Of course, he naturally recalls the painting. It is implied that it can be purchased at a moderate figure, but the owner does not wish to make it known that he is short of money. Then we set the figure. It is quite high, perhaps several thousand dollars, and the terms are that half of the sum shall be paid before delivery and half on receipt. Of course, the first half of the figure is our profit. We will not see the second half, we do not wish to do so. So the American pays the fifty per cent. The picture will be delivered at such and such a time. We arrange to have the Rembrandt delivered by an ordinary service. By express mail we send a cutting of the newspaper report of the robbery and a photograph of the Rembrandt. The American is in a dilemma, he is not sure whether the picture is the one which was stolen. On the other hand, he does not want his name to be mixed up in any scandal. He does not wish to get in touch with the former owner. Touché! He either hides the picture or he courteously returns it, and he writes off the money which he has paid.'

In the general run the forger remains anonymous and within the organization I have been writing about he is certainly well looked after. Now and then, however, a forger will feel impelled to assert himself, if only to show that he is just as good as 'they' are. Such a man is David Stein, who is one of the most successful forgers of recent years. In 1969 he was sentenced to eighteen months' imprisonment in America, but so good was his work in the modern idiom that the Wright Hepburn Gallery of London put him under a two-year contract. At a first exhibition at the Halkin Arcade, London, his forty-seven paintings were sold for 5,500 guineas by the morning after the opening. Stein paints 'in the style of the moderns', and while in prison in America he produced a number of neo-Rouaults. After his fame spread he started signing his own name on his canvases.

Not all the people in the 'passing off' trade achieve the fame of David Stein. Indeed, they have no wish for fame, and this is nowhere more pronounced than in the lesser but fairly new business of coloured prints. These are simply black and white prints taken from old books, hand coloured and then framed before being sold for up to ten guineas or more. The profit is huge and the deception blatant to anybody who knows the difference between modern mineral-based colours and genuine antique lithographic hues, which are much softer.

To the layman it must seem incredible that the high-class art forger should go to such lengths and pains to achieve a convincing authenticity. If they 'went legitimate' in industry, many of them would probably rise high in the field of research and development. Of course, most of them are so idiosyncratic that they would not last very long. Ivan, for instance, would need a laboratory to himself, unlimited funds and *carte blanche* to pursue his own projects, which are many and varied, although his main source of income comes from the manufacture of paper for incunabula. To understand this highly esoteric section of the rare book trade it is first necessary to know something about the meaning of the word itself. It refers to books printed before 1501. There are relatively few private collectors of incunabula, but the advantage is that they are all moneyed and they all suffer to a greater or lesser degree from the collecting instinct.

Ivan is self-taught in everything, and his present activities are the result of an early training in industrial chemistry. His father came from the Baltic, his mother was English, and the individual temperaments manifested themselves in their son. He interrupted his studies to join the RAF, flying with distinction in the Far East. His father left quite a lot of money and, after his mother died in 1950, he found that he had no particular responsibilities, and so he set up as an unqualified consultant chemist, tackling technical problems for many minor firms which were just getting on their feet. He did quite well for a time and then found that what he was giving was an uneconomical service, he was charging too little for too much, and, because he was not a very good business man, he pursued most of his jobs far beyond their logical conclusion. This went on for three years until he was visited by a gentleman from Belgium who had offices in The Hague. He said that he was in the business of papermaking for limited editions. Ivan happened to have a passing interest in papermaking, and believed that he could produce one or two reports for his client. Some months later he did produce something new in rag paper manufacture, and he was paid £1,500 on the nail. In the bargain he was given a free trip to The Hague to stay with his client at a comfortable flat in the city. It was then that he was, to put it politely, propositioned. His client made no secret of the fact that his main interest lay in producing paper which would not only look pre-1500 but also stand up to any test.

As soon as he got back to London Ivan analysed several specimens, which his client had supplied, and quickly found that they consisted of cotton and linen. Taking lengths of the modern equivalent, he plunged them into water baths and mashed them up with bleaches of his own devising. When the 'porrage' was just right he smeared it on frames and dried it off, using a hair drier. He went on experimenting for six months, tossing one crumpled batch after another into the waste bin, but he did finally start making what was to all intents and purposes a medieval paper. He also found ways and means of watermarking it, using a hot metal die. His client, who had left him to it, now reappeared, and he was delighted, even when he found that it cost £25 per sheet to produce in terms of time and materials. Ivan was rewarded with a steady job, running a small plant to produce medieval paper. After a long period of research and hard work, however, he wanted his independence and said so. He was quite willing to make and sell the paper, but that was as far as it could go. This exasperated his client, who seemed to visualize a little factory producing rare antiquarian books on an assembly-line basis. The key was, of course, paper. Without that the business could not exist and it was obvious that a compromise must be found. Ivan eventually said that he would supply as much paper as would be required at £15 per folio sheet. At the present time the order is running at up to 50 sheets per week and most of it is being stored in the Netherlands. Ivan seems to be quite satisfied with an average of £750 a week, and he does all the work at his place in the Home Counties. There is nothing illegal in this, as he is at pains to point out, despite the fact that he often fabricates watermarks taken from 'Les Filigranes' published in Geneva, 1907, which is the standard work on watermarks from 1282 to 1600.

What of the paper itself? Once it is decided to manufacture a specific title which is fairly rare, a London buyer is detailed to locate and buy a copy. This sounds easy but it is far from being that, because the semi-rare incunabula is much more difficult to find than the item which is extremely rare. To the professional London scout who is well known to such firms as Maggs, Myers and Rota, also to the cataloguers at Hodgsons, the antiquarian book saleroom, it can generally be done within three or four weeks. The regular price is paid, and this can be up to £1,000 or even more. The item goes by courier to The Hague, and from then on it is a matter for the expert forgers who can create anything from Dürer engravings to antique typefaces. The leather for the binding comes from Antwerp, where the organization holds large stocks for just this purpose. Leather is a subject in itself, and the methods of making it look over 500 years old are complicated, involving acids, waxes and rollered machines which impart exactly the right amount of wear.

These forgeries are not singles, they are produced several dozen at a time, and intermediaries pass them off simultaneously at several dozen centres throughout the world. It is difficult to obtain any idea of the profits, but if you think in terms of, say, forty copies at about £250 each, the gross figure is in the region of £10,250, although the organization occasionally feels sufficiently ambitious to produce some really choice and expensive items with a paper value of between £750 to £1,000 each. But that is the big stuff and producing and marketing it calls for months of work at craftsman level. Students of this kind of fraud have often commented on the fact that for all the trouble it takes and the need for the skills of qualified craftsmen, the game is not really worth the candle. But it obviously depends on what one expects to get out of it. The organization at The Hague must have spent vast sums on the development of resources, and they reckon to create up to one thousand first-class forgeries a year. It is seldom that prices drop below the £100 per copy level. There is, of course, a limit to the number of incunabula which can be launched without raising suspicions. In order to avoid such difficulties, the organization recently started producing reproductions of classical erotica, which is a collectors' staple throughout the world. These sell at up to £250 a volume. Another variation is the production of fragments of pages, each supposedly from a famous volume. Rare genuine fragments command extremely high prices in the London and New York salerooms, and many a collector will write a cheque for what he believes to be a page from the Gutenberg Bible or some such rarity.

If paintings and rare books are among the most difficult items to falsify to the degree where they will take in the expert collector, coins are among the easiest. The first professional coiner I ever met was shortly after the war in Cairo. R—— was a Rumanian, part of the driftwood of war, cynical about politics, a bit of a Fascist in his outlook, and his family had been landowners for centuries. He was the last of the line. Day after day he sat in the Polar Bar, drinking iced lager and the occasional whisky. I could not understand how he managed to live in his opulent flat with a servant and a car. At that time Cairo was a fairly expensive city and it was only now beginning to recover from the war and attract tourists. R—— looked at me with irritation on his face. Was it any business of mine how he lived? No, I said apologetically, but one liked to know about one's friends. At the mention of 'friends', his eyes lit up. It was many years since he had a friend. One reached a point of not needing friends, simply a resourcefulness, that was all. At that time my work did not concern the circles in which R—— moved, we were bar acquaintances and that was all. All the same, he was critical of my security. I was a British citizen while he was stateless and in Egypt he was at the pleasure of Farouk's government which was, at that time, unstable. He seemed to be the sort of man who needed to confide in somebody. As it happened, all he wanted to do was boast, and this form of self-indulgence can be extremely tedious when it comes from an unshaven, overweight character like R——, but I put up with it for several more weeks. In the end he invited me to his flat for a meal. I decided to go.

His boy prepared cous-cous, and while we were waiting for the table to be set, we drank straight gin as an aperitif. I could not help noticing a collection of ancient coins laid out on a piece of red velvet on a circular table near the balcony where the evening sun struck them, making them gleam. After more gin I asked his permission to look more closely at them. He had been waiting for this moment, and urged me to handle them. As I did so, he told me their histories. This was Roman and that was a coin of the Renaissance, and this . . . but even without any knowledge of coins, I quickly realized that this modest collection must be worth a lot of money, because every exhibit was in such beautiful condition. In view of their age, many were worn, of course, but their general excellence was quite breathtaking. If it was not presumptuous and strictly between friends, I said, what might their value be? He took his time replying, and then said very seriously that the value would be no more than approximately two hundred piastres. At that time the piastre was worth $2\frac{1}{2}d$, so this made a total of £2 1*s* 8*d*. I refrained from commenting, and we were well into our cous-cous when he burst out laughing. The question must have been plain on my face, and he eventually admitted that these were simply replicas of his father's collection, the only tangible assets which he had managed to bring out of Europe as a displaced person. At first he did consider selling the lot for whatever he could get for them, but offers were few because they were not of general interest at that time. It takes time and civilization to create values. He starved for a time and soon after arriving in Cairo via the Lebanon he found the market much improved. He then went to the trouble of learning the art of casting in precious metals and gold plating from a Jewish goldsmith in a workshop halfway between Cairo and Heliopolis, and they came to an arrangement to cover the cost of tuition by splitting the profits from sales of the first batch. Master copies were made and it was from these that replicas were made, using the ancient 'lost wax' method, an adaptation of a system first used in 328 B.C. Lost wax is valuable as a method because, while it takes a little longer than other methods, such as centrifuging, it ensures a flawless facsimile of the impression taken from the master.

A man like R—— may be the leading figure in an organization which now periodically floods the London, Paris, Berlin and New York markets with spurious antique coins and, in all probability, the nineteenth-century seals and rings, for they all lend themselves to the process which he described to me in detail.

The prices of many antique coins are not high, but, on the other hand, it costs remarkably little to produce such a small object. If it is cast solid in gold or other metal, then the job can be done in a single stage, especially if the centrifugal method is used, by which means coins can be made on a more or less repetition basis. If the coin is to be cast in one metal and plated in another, then it costs less but takes longer, because it must pass through several processes. Amongst the favourite targets of forgers are the silver Coronation medal of James II after the Dutch engraver, Johann (or John) Roettier, dating from 1685. It is, of course, essential that an impression is made direct from an authentic coin or medal. One would not, for instance, risk flooding the market with 1871 half-crown pieces. Only two are known and, in fact, no half-crowns were officially struck from 1851 to 1873, but a few were made in 1868 and other years. Any half-crown of this period is naturally suspect and authentication is generally sought direct from the Royal Mint.

London is one of the most crowded centres for the creation of fakes of all kinds, from sculpture to furniture, and it is possible to secure the services of craftsmen in practically any line, right down to the man who will cheerfully reproduce Edwardian and Victorian ivory and ebony handles for walking sticks. But this is not his first source of revenue, because he makes about £3,000 a year out of Oriental netsuke, many of which find their way into provincial salerooms and antique shops, where they can fetch up to £150 or £200. It is his wife who does the actual passing off, posing as a widow who wants to sell her 'late husband's' possessions which he brought back from the East. She has already had them valued, she explains, but does not expect to receive the full price. Up to 15 netsuke a week are sold during the winter months, the summer being spent carving them. The man who makes them complains about the lack of suitably aged ivory, for even a small piece now costs £12. At a pinch, he will use old billiard balls, although he pays frequent visits to Friedlein, the ivory merchants in the Minories in London.

There is a dear old soul in West London who has made a lifetime study of lace-making to the extent of spending several years in the main centres of Paris, Milan, Venice, Chantilly and Genoa, studying all the techniques employed. She knows the famous Jacoby-Ikle collection in the Museum of Industries and Crafts at St Gall, Switzerland, better than the curator. During her travels she met the lace forgers of Italy, where the trade runs in the family for generations. The intermediaries come from the cities to pick up the goods and pay spot cash. So traditional is lace forgery in many of the villages about twenty miles from Milan and Rome that it is practically beyond perfection, being a direct copy of the convent-made Rosaline lace, which is sold to the tourists as 'antique'. Even the expert is completely taken in, because the Rosaline replica always incorporates the many tiny faults which are evident in hand work. But simply making the lace in traditional patterns and using materials which happen to be very close to the antique real thing is not by any means the end of it, because it has to be boiled for hours on end and certain oils are added to give the appearance of venerable age. The lady in London has made thousands of yards of Rosaline lace. In the early days she tried to sell it as her own work to fashionable London stores, but she had the same experience as craft-workers elsewhere who find that stores will pay only a pittance yet sell at a vast profit. Lace-making was her only talent, and so she had no alternative but to copy the methods of the Italian lace-makers and forgers, and she nowadays makes mantillas and shawls, giving them the prolonged boiling treatment in her washing machine until the antique appearance materializes. She spin dries them and then, after another process to age the lace, she sets off to spin the yarn in antique shops all over the country. The better-class dealer who knows very little about lace is most often taken in when she represents herself to be an impoverished widow, and some of them will pay up to £60 for a large shawl, although she is always careful not to go back there again. The forgery of classical lace represents a highly lucrative field for craftsmen or craftswomen. The only snag seems to be that it takes a lifetime to know how to produce the authentic effect.

A somewhat easier material than lace is clay, and it is one of the favourites in ceramics and the manufacture of terracotta primitives. Provided the modelling is right, and the firing has been done correctly, it would take a museum chemist to determine whether a piece is a forgery or authentic. A great many of the primitive clay objects in the national collections, such as the British Museum, are said to be forgeries. Oriental glazed dishes are produced at a modern pottery, and the now favoured Staffordshire dogs are turned out, some with a genuine-looking mark and others without any sign of origin. There is no doubt that certain West End dealers who specialize in porcelain figures may occasionally have through their hands the figures which are made by an exceptionally talented young man who cannot make a legitimate living as a potter. His Meissen pieces, complete with the famous crossed swords mark, have gone in their dozens to America.

Rather larger in scale is furniture. Amongst my earlier instructional manuals was one on the finishing of wood, and in the text I gave the formula of the Chippendale workshops, involving the sieving of rottenstone through silk, then mixing the dust with certain oils and, finally, the treatment of the wood itself. It was evidently a useful tip as far as at least one workshop was concerned, where a great deal of Chippendale is made for what the proprietor described as 'the classy trade'. They had for a long time been worried about the surface finish of their pieces, although the dealers who accepted it had no worries. Many of these pieces were placed with householders who earned a small commission by advertising them in local papers and selling to private buyers and dealers. By this means six craftsmen working as a kind of industrial co-operative were able to achieve a gross turnover between £800 and £1,250 a week. Not that they worked every week, because the enterprise was sufficiently profitable for them to work only alternate weeks throughout the summer months.

The man who started it all was at some pains to explain that he and his colleagues were all highly qualified cabinet makers. But for the fact that the furniture industry had become what he called 'a matter of stapling orange-box wood together', they would have stayed on at the factories. So great was their interest in fine furniture that they enlisted the aid of a business manager, who put together the organization for passing off Chippendale chairs and other pieces.

'We don't use just any wood. We use old wood out of buildings that are being taken down. We've got a warehouse full of oak, walnut, mahogany and God knows what. We don't use a mixture of old wood and new wood, like certain people I could tell you about. Our stuff is all good old wood, all the way through. A lot of hard work goes into everything we do. I was down the V. and A. (Victoria and Albert Museum), going round their furniture department till I was blue in the face. I got museum photos of most of their stuff. That's better than a drawing, but they reckon Chippendale published his own pattern books. I've got some booksellers on the look out for them, but no luck so far. Tell you what broke my heart when we got started first of all. We made these three chairs and they were lovely, then our manager comes up and says yes, yes, very nice, they look just like brand new antiques, don't they? I asked him what he meant, and he said they'll have to be knocked about a bit, chip a bit off here and there, then repair it and make it look as though it's been repaired, otherwise we'll be in schtuck. That's what we did, we marked them and chipped them and Christ alive, we were so fed up with what we'd done that we went to the boozer after that. But our manager was very pleased and he got rid of them for nearly £100 each. We've done a lot better since then. We're used to it now.'

Until recent times the fraudulent art market did not include much in the way of sculpture in wood, stone and metal, but this is now coming along very well, and a start seems to have been made in Germany, for I have on my shelves some excellent forgeries, all of them from a little factory near Dortmund. One is in the Italian style, the head of a young boy. From a distance it looks entirely authentic, but it is, in fact, made from crushed semi-precious stone mixed with a bonding medium. The other two are cast from a stone-like substance, one being a Hellenic fragment of a female face, the other is Chacmool, the Mexican rain god.

Most of the wood sculpture which is now being passed off, knowingly or unknowingly, by dealers, is in the Gothic idiom, the best of it ornamented with fine gilding and colouring, for the Gothic artist always coloured a carving, and it was not until the great Tilmann Riemenschneider (1460–1531) appeared in Germany that the wood was left in its natural state. Carving and colouring were probably the result of a partnership between carver and artist, and even now, so I am informed by Gino Masero, the authority on the subject, carving and finishing represent different functions in the commercial carving shop.

Nowadays the most accomplished carver forgers are tucked away in the country, where they pursue their delicate craft unsuspected by the neighbours. It would obviously be dangerous to work on such pieces in a city studio where callers may be frequent and curiosity would be aroused. A line drawn down the middle of a map of the British Isles with another across the country on a parallel with Nottingham would pass through the bungalow and garden shed of Alfred. He is paying off his mortgage and supporting a wife and two children solely by means of a set of tools which he made for himself. At one time he worked as a porter in a famous London saleroom and he was, even then, interested in wood sculpture and wood carving. In conversation with an art historian, he learned that modern carving tools are quite different from those used by the craftsmen of Gothic times, and this accounted for a radical difference in styles. The historian said that it would be impossible to carve in the Gothic manner, using modern tools. Alfred started doing some private research in the subject, and he traced some illustrations of old tools. This enabled him to make a set of carving tools, which resembled miniature axes, all very rudimentary and apparently clumsy. He had already done a lot of carving with modern tools, but the new approach offered great possibilities. After two years of hard work, he finally fell into the Gothic idiom and was able to produce several large heads of Christ and innumerable Apostles in addition to one or two reliefs, although his 'agent' finds it difficult to get rid of the bigger pieces, because they are expensive and they take weeks to complete due to the limited working space in his garden shed. The technique of true Gothic reproduction is to make the sculpture in several pieces, just as the original craftsman used to do, and then peg them together. Alfred is not very creative, he is a copyist, but he is still an exceptionally fine craftsman. His 'agent' takes about 45 per cent of the profits, but he somehow manages to sell Alfred's entire output sooner or later, occasionally complaining about the length of time it takes to achieve the antique effect which include convincing worm holes, tracing of coloration and gilding and abraded surfaces. It is possible that the 'agent' is doing rather better out of it than Alfred cares to believe, but the craftsman says that he is quite satisfied and it is better than working in a saleroom.

This is no place to pass judgment on art frauds and forgeries. I can only report on the people I know and their methods. Without doubt they are all accomplished artists, many of them more talented than many practitioners of modern art, and few of them are dependent upon mere copying but are creative in their own right. However, it strikes me as being a sad trade, because few of these people are as wealthy as the people who sell their products. But then, it has been the same story for centuries.

Chapter Six

Cheque Counter Cheque

There is no international organization which is devoted entirely to studying and sharing out the *modus operandi* of fraud and white-collar crime. If such an organization were to exist, one thing would soon become quite evident, namely that conmen tend to be derivative. This means that an accomplished operator will practice and perfect a particular method of making money and he will stick to the same method for the rest of his criminal life, regardless of whether he goes to prison for months or years at a time or remains undetected. There is a noticeable lack of versatility on the part of the average operator which somehow compels him to go round and round in his treadmill. One man admitted to me: 'It's all I know, it's probably the only thing I can do really well, so why should I change?' He was fifty-five years of age and had served fifteen years in three different terms for the same type of offence. The only drawback to his brand of artisan philosophy is that once the pattern has been detected and labelled and then attached to the individual operator, the operator is bound to suffer detection and imprisonment from time to time. The Fraud Squad attaches far greater importance to the *modus operandi* than to fingerprints. Basically, all methods are known, even if they do materialize under different names from time to time. From the police point of view the difficulty lies in detecting them early enough to frighten off the operator. But at best frightening him off can only be a temporary measure. Few crooks desist for long. They are like warehouse mice, gnawing at the sacks of grain, and if they are flushed away from one sack, they will only go on elsewhere and find another sack. The persistence of such criminals represents a fascinating study. Even when given the opportunity of going straight and holding down a regular job, the majority of them will eventually drift back into crime, despite the fact that it is far from being an easy life. The average habitual criminal lives on the razor-edge of being picked up and questioned. Even when he is 'resting' at the time, there is a nagging fear—and it may be justified—that the police will pin something on him. This applies particularly in the densely populated cities where the crime problem is mountainous and an offence of some kind is committed every few minutes. Nobody has yet achieved a correlation between the numerical strength of the police versus the numerical strength of criminals, but in cities like London, Berlin and New York the odds are in favour of the criminal, due quite simply to a superior strength of numbers. A prime example is the fact that something like 75 per cent of all theft goes unsolved. In white-collar crime and fraud the unsolved rate must be even greater for the simple reason that most of it goes unreported and therefore unknown, except to the victims themselves. In fraud and confidence trickery the pickings are easier, too. The polished conman differs drastically from the common thief. He is an ingenious creature, a pleasure to talk to and often with a good education behind him, although this is not always the case. He gets high marks for a strong stomach and sheer nerve, too, for he often has to give a performance which must be sustained for months on end, whereas the car thief needs nerve for only brief periods at a time. Despite his interesting qualities, the conman has not been the subject of any profound studies by sociologists or criminologists, although I did know one psychiatrist who was determined to find out what made a conman tick, and he wound up practically writing a cheque for shares in a firm which did not exist. It says a lot for the conman. Properly channelled, he could be an asset to any department of the persuasion industry. Yet oddly enough the conmen I have met have always been as gullible as anybody else when it comes to the wiles of advertising and the brainwashing techniques practised by governments and political parties.

One inevitable conclusion which can be drawn from this is that the conman will continue to flourish long after the unlikely event of all other crooks being locked up in their cells. It seems to be quite impossible to eradicate the habits of some members of the population who painlessly remove cash or goods from other members of the community. As in other spheres of life, the cost of living in crime keeps pace with the economic spiral elsewhere. By and large, fraud and white-collar crime increases at a much faster rate, and this is due in part to the very nature of the work of the Fraud Squad. It generally takes some time before the victims of a fraud smell a rat, and it is even longer before any of them pluck up enough courage to report the facts. The more the victim loses, the longer he hesitates before admitting his own stupidity. In a complicated swindle the facts take a long time to accumulate, and even when they have been put together, it is unlikely that the police will be able to act at once. In any police department the Fraud Squad is so overworked that they may be unable to clear the matter up in a reasonable time, and so that particular file may well go to the bottom of the pile. Fraud investigation is notoriously complicated, it takes a lot of time to get at the truth, and so the relatively small fraud case must wait. It is fortunate that the small-time conman rarely flees to Bermuda but cheerfully goes on mulcting a new victim.

If any rules govern the con-game, they were all broken by Mr X, an absolute amateur but a masterly one. The nature of this book being what it is, I have no alternative but to refer to him by this pseudonym, which may well irritate the reader. However, I am calling him Mr X not to protect the man himself or the banks concerned but the author and the publisher. I hope that the reader will be sufficiently acquainted with the law of libel to bear with me.

At first sight Mr X was everything which many of us would like to be. He was essentially a man of the City, agreeable and cultured, obviously moneyed. He was likeable and he was helpful. I had borrowed five pounds from him in an emergency, and, when I returned it less than a day later, he gave me a cigar and said that I need not have bothered. After all, he made more than £3,000 a year as a shipping broker and he could afford a fiver or so any time I wanted it, he said. When I first got to know him, he was coming to the end of his days in the City, due to circumstances which he described in detail after we got to know each other rather better. I liked his bland open face as he blinked at me over a cocktail at a London party. It was one of those affairs where City men mingle agreeably with television people and starlets, and the conversation is always desultory and low-toned. Nobody ever seems to know who is giving the party or why, but such things do not matter, because they rarely last more than a couple of totally pointless hours. There is no obligation to thank the host or consider returning the invitation. Due to the fact that Mr X and I shared the same opinion of such functions, we left early and I suggested a drink at the *Running Footman*. This is a Mayfair pub at one end of Hays Mews, just off Berkeley Square, and it is always an interesting place if only because members of Buckingham Palace domestic staff are in the habit of having a quiet drink there in the evenings, and you can occasionally hear gossip about the Prince and Her. Mr X had never been there before. All his pubs were down Bishopsgate and Clerkenwell way, he said, and I must come and have a look at them one of these days. He was drinking whisky and he did not seem to be in any hurry to go home. In passing he did mention that he was living alone after two unfortunate marriages. He was, he added a few moments later, a poor hand at marriage. When I asked him about his work he said that he had been in brokerage ever since leaving public school, starting as a clerk and eventually making enough money to buy himself a junior partnership. Five or six years later he raised several thousand pounds to buy his way into a more important firm, and he had been there ever since.

He was the kind of man who talks very easily and yet says remarkably little. Even his curiosity about me was very much *en passant*. When I mentioned that I was in medicine, he merely nodded and said that it must be quite interesting. He was like a dusty mirror which presents a predictable but very fuzzy reflection. As we sat there, drinking, I came to the conclusion that he was just one of those people you bump into at a party and that was about all you could say about him. Had I been gifted with more insight, I would have recalled the saying about things not always being what they seem to be. But at that moment there was no reason to question their validity. In retrospect, I have no doubt that he was not at that time seriously considering a career as a conman. He was the last man in the world for it. One of the characteristics of the professional conman is that he will deliberately cultivate anybody who may fit into his plan, and he will often ask a lot of probing questions in an obvious manner. While he is going about this he is casting people to play roles in the little comedy which he is mentally writing. There was nothing like that with Mr X. He became a lone operator and he did not require a supporting cast. All the same, I did feel curious when he phoned me at the hospital a week later and suggested that we have another drink. And so I accepted. We could meet at his house, he said, and carefully spelled out an address in north London.

It turned out to be the kind of house which I have often wanted to own, a large red brick edifice put up in the 'thirties by a master builder, carefully detached from its neighbours by a six-foot privet hedge. The double gates were wrought iron, painted in two colours, and a carved wooden number plate was held in position by a styled iron bracket. The edges of the contoured lawn which bordered the macadam drive were marked out with blue and white chippings. Altogether, it was a splendid residence with huge bay windows and heavy velvet curtains.

He made me very welcome, busying himself with two stainless steel platters of canapés and large measures of whisky. He had gone to the trouble of getting the canapés in town, he said. Living on his own, and relying on a daily help, any form of advanced catering was a bit beyond him. He hoped I did not mind the somewhat Spartan refreshments. I assured him that I was quite happy, noticing that there was something slightly different about him tonight, as though he was absolutely determined to play the part of the host. Every now and then he sat down for a few moments, but never for long because he kept finding things to do. First it was a cheroot. I must try one of his cheroots. And could he freshen up my drink? Then he started talking about an oil painting on the wall. He had bought it on impulse from a gallery, but still could not make head or tail of it, because it was so modern. Did I know anything about art? After we had exhausted the enigmatic nature of modern art forms, he suggested that we trot along to a nearby pub for a couple of steaks. When I said that I was not really hungry, he muttered that there was no point in eating for the sake of eating. He slumped down in a chair and gave me a wistful smile. 'I'm terribly sorry. But the fact is, I don't entertain at home at all these days. When you are on your own, you just don't bother. I generally spend an evening at the club. Are you on your own?' When I said that I often had far too much company around me, he nodded. 'Really? So you'd rather be alone, would you? I know precisely how you must feel. Told you about my two marriages, didn't I? I'm just not cut out for marriage—I wish I'd realized that fact years ago . . .'

Then he started telling me about the first marriage at an early age, when he was egged on by his parents to propose to a pretty and very stupid girl with a petulant temper. There were no children because she was honest enough to say that she did not want a physical relationship. That put the tin hat on the traditional image of marital bliss as far as he was concerned. A few years later he deliberately deserted her and she divorced him, and so he married again, this time an older woman, but it collapsed after eighteen months. He seemed to feel better after telling me about it.

We sat there in a conversational no-man's land until he started off again. It was age this time. He was conscious of the fact that he was not getting any younger. 'I feel the pressure, you know, especially in business, and things are changing in my firm.' It appeared that his little company was developing a new image. He was the oldest partner, which might explain why the others had not consulted him about the proposed changes and alterations. Brokerage, he said, was a peculiar business. While many firms still lived on contracts drafted more than twenty years ago, the new firms found it hard to get on their feet, and so they had to try and diversify to make ends meet. Not that his firm was in serious difficulties. Sound as a rock. The trouble was the attitude of the younger men. 'They always want to dabble and I just don't like dabbling. You can lose your shirt. Perhaps I'm a bit over-cautious, but in my view we ought to work up more long-term contracts. I mean, you've only got to look at the state of merchant banking. More losses than gains in that sector, I'm sure.' He embarked on a long and rather pointless story about a firm of merchant bankers which was engaged in backing the smoked fish industry, and he followed it up with a string of City anecdotes, all of which seemed to endorse his dislike of change for the sake of change. From the Rock of Ages appearance of his house, I was beginning to appreciate that the building complemented the character of its owner.

Several more weeks passed by. I had almost forgotten about him. We were suddenly very busy at the hospital. One day, when I was coming to the end of fourteen hours' exhausting work, the reception desk phoned to say that Mr X had called to see me. I asked them to tell him that I was very busy. He offered to wait until I was available, and we could perhaps have a bite together. I took my time about showering and dressing, wondering all the time what was wrong with this man. He seemed to explode into my life whenever he felt like it, and I could not muster much feeling for him one way or the other.

We went to a Jewish restaurant where I initiated him into the pleasures of hot salt beef. This time he seemed to have much more confidence in himself and I thought that I had misjudged him, because he talked freely and with greater confidence. Towards the end of the meal he announced: 'Well, I've finally decided to retire—'

'Have you now? You're still a bit young for it,' I pointed out. 'I suppose it's been forced on you. That situation in your firm—'

'Oh, a bit of both, really. I'm in my late fifties, you know, even if I don't look it. But you're quite right. I can't stand the firm any longer. They've forced my hand and the atmosphere—well, I can tell you in confidence, it's changed for the worse. I'd be surprised if they can carry on for five years. They keep having meetings behind my back, making decisions, and they don't even have the courtesy to mention it.'

'Sure you're not imagining it?' I asked obviously.

'I know it sounds paranoid, but I tell you it's going on. I'm perfectly entitled to know what's happening, aren't I? I'm a partner or I'm not a partner. Dammit, they're using some of my money, don't you forget it.'

'All I can say is I'm glad I'm not in business.' Finishing my coffee, I asked: 'You'll be keeping your house on, will you?'

He calmed down. 'Yes, for a bit, anyway. Nice place, cost a lot of money, but it's all paid for. It's a place to go home to. Well, there it is. I thought you'd be interested to know . . . you're a jolly good listener. I don't know many people. Had to tell somebody . . .'

At this point we should step into Mr X's shoes, because the subsequent events can be related only in his own words, just as he told them to me nearly three years later. After our meal in the Jewish restaurant he disappeared from view, and when he finally popped up again, I had changed my area of work. He managed to trace me through a professional association to which I belonged. As we shook hands I said that he looked much slimmer, and he explained that he had been in prison. He now intended going to live in France, so he thought he would look me up to say goodbye, because I was the only person he really knew, and he hoped I didn't mind.

During the next eight hours he told me the whole story.

'One thing I did learn was to get my priorities right. If we could all be taught how to plan our priorities, life would become much easier, but we muddle along, that's the trouble, we just muddle and muddle, and we hope everything will sort itself out.

'My life has always been uncomfortable, you know. I've always been afraid of things. Death, for instance. I've always been scared stiff of death, the actual thought of dying, although they tell me you go into some sort of a coma and you don't know anything about it. That's the trouble, though, I really do want to know about it, then if I did I wouldn't be so frightened.

'There was always a lot of death in my family. Aunts and uncles seemed to pop off practically every year, because we were a very big family, and so they all aged together and they all seemed to die together, and I suppose there must be a whole generation of my cousins, all growing old together, but I don't keep in touch with any of them, so I don't really know. My Uncle Charles was the first and he had a rather grand funeral. I'll always remember his funeral. He actually had a hearse drawn by horses. It caused quite a stir. They said it was the last of the horse funerals. But he'd actually laid it down in his will and it just had to be done. Yes, they managed to get horses for Uncle Charles. It may sound unhealthy, but I took a morbid interest in all those deaths. I was the favourite nephew, you see. It made me play up to them. In the end it was their legacies that paid for most of my education. I had about £2,000 in my account by the time I graduated—it was quite a lot of money in those days. But those legacies did me a disservice, because they altered my outlook, my perspective, because I somehow got the idea that security was represented by cash at the bank. That was probably the worst idea I ever had, but it was pumped into me that cash and property were a number one priority. My father must have read a lot of Galsworthy, because he was always talking about it and all he ever looked at in a newspaper was the City page. So the idea of security seemed to lodge in my mind, it became part of the scheme of things. That's one of the reasons why I bought the house. My father would have approved of me doing that. He'd have seen it as an investment rather than a home.

'Do you know what happens when you get security minded? You start getting other ideas—about standards, for instance. Keeping up standards, that kind of thing. It sounds so stupid nowadays. Dressing for dinner and all that kind of thing. My second wife was frightfully keen on it. We had to know the right kind of people, eat the right kind of food, discuss the right kind of books. We were so damned superior, you know, that I wonder how we managed to breathe the right kind of air! She built a kind of strait-jacket of living for me, and I was fool enough to believe she was right. I was very weak about it. Even sex . . . well, you can imagine what sex was like. It's probably the only thing she ever gave up and that was because I didn't quite conform. I couldn't conform. I'd got what she called lower tastes. She was very conventional when it came to sex. I remember once, when I suggested she keep her dress on but didn't wear any undies, she gave me a very strange look when I said I got more satisfaction that way. She said I ought to see a doctor about it . . .

'Well, you remember the situation in the firm? I told you all about it. It really did prey on my mind. But the snag to getting out was simply a lack of capital. Over the years I'd secured far too much of my money in annuities and investments, simply because it seemed to be the thing to do. When I came to look into it, I had a dickens of a lot of money tied up. I really couldn't see much chance of buying into another partnership, either. In brokerage the snag is that generations come and generations go, and by the time you are over fifty, you've just about had it. No use pretending otherwise. I had £4,600 in the bank, and the very first thing I did was sell my car. It was no good to me, standing in the garage, and I never used it. I got £400 for it, and so that made a total of £5,100 in the bank. Now, if you invest that kind of sum, you only get a pittance in interest. Even the best of the investment trusts don't offer a high enough dividend to warrant locking up a large sum for a guaranteed term, especially now that money is losing its value all the time. My need was a steady income, and I just couldn't live without one. I even thought about starting a business of some kind, doing something really independent, but in the end I couldn't see any future in that, either, and I knew I'd have gone bust in a year or two, simply for lack of experience . . .

'Have you ever tried making a decision on your own, without anybody to talk to about it? You don't know if you're doing right or wrong, there's no way of telling. That's the fix I was in. I had £5,100 tucked away in the bank, living in a house worth, I suppose, about £12,000, and I simply didn't know which way to turn. I was seriously worried about my future. It was absolutely ludicrous at my age. If I lived another twenty years, I'd certainly have to sell the house or else raise a second mortgage or else move into a smaller place on a reduced income, and I didn't want to do anything like that. You see—the same old bogy was there about keeping up standards. You can't get away from it, you know.

'Of course, if I hadn't been to prison, I wouldn't be telling you all this, would I? But the queer thing is that I wanted to tell you, not because what I did was successful, but simply because I did it and it worked out all right and I planned it on my own. I'd never had any what you might call unconventional ideas before. I remember, I was quite shocked when my firm inadvertently got mixed up in some little shipping fiddle. We were the innocent party, but the day it dawned on us that somebody had set out quite deliberately to defraud us and several other brokers, I was genuinely shocked and horrified. I was really righteous. It's rum the way things work out, though. Less than two years later there I was, working out a way of robbing a bank. And it wasn't going to be the usual kind of robbery, either. Oh no, I'd made my mind up about that. I was going to do it without any violence or bloodshed. I was going to be civilized about it. You see, standards again, even in a matter like that. The truth of it was, I didn't want to offend anybody, and to a certain extent it did work out like that, although there was inevitably a certain amount of unpleasantness towards the end.

'Now I look back on it, it does seem incredible. The reason why I made the actual decision was much the same as that thing about Hilary climbing Everest, because it was there, and I did want negotiable currency, actual cash which I could use to live on. I even fixed the capital sum which I would need to see me through to the age of about seventy-five. Mind you, I've changed my mind now, because I think I shall need more.

'I was quite obviously not the type of chap who marches into a bank and produces a gun and a bag and tells the clerk to fill it up or else. I could never do a thing like that. I'd faint or something. That was why I spent week after week, working out all the details, and when I was quite sure it was absolutely foolproof, I resigned from my firm. I can still remember every detail of that morning. I went in early and drafted my resignation, and I made quite sure that I claimed my share of the profits on an annual basis, regardless of the circumstances, because I knew it would give me something to fall back on, although I was fairly sure the firm would fail sooner or later. Then I went to see the senior partner. You know, business is such a heartless affair! I'd been there several years, I owned a chunk of the firm, I'd helped to build things up and keep the wheels turning, but they just accepted my resignation without a murmur. Perhaps they'd been expecting it or they wanted to ease me out. Anyway, they took it and didn't even say the conventional thing, and when my time was up I took the four of them out to dinner on my last evening.

We were all very civilized about it, but there wasn't a single word of commiseration or even a question about what I intended doing with myself. You'd think they'd have asked. So I thought, oh well, to hell with the lot of you, and off I went. But it just goes to show, you needn't expect any human feelings in business. I was relieved to get out of it in the end.

'A few days later I closed my personal account with the City bank where I'd been banking for years, and I walked out with £5,100 packed in my briefcase. It didn't take up much space. I had a rather peculiar morning. I had a cup of coffee somewhere and as I had no change on me I pulled out a bundle of notes and took one off the top to pay for what I'd had. At first I didn't have a single idea what to do with myself, so I went and sat in Hyde Park with the briefcase at my feet, and I somehow got talking to an old woman. She told me her life story. It was very sad, about the way she'd lost her husband and three sons, and she kept telling me about how she was all alone, as though she was proud of it. Then she thanked me for listening and said she must have bored me, and I said not at all, and off she went. I sat and watched her going slowly down the gravel path and for a time I couldn't help wondering what was wrong with us all. She was an old woman I'd never seen before and I wouldn't see again, and she'd told me all about her terrible life, and she wasn't to know she was talking to a man who intended robbing a bank. Up to that time I'd still got a choice, of course. I even started thinking about looking for a job and registering with one of the executive placement agencies, but after I'd looked at the advertisements in the newspapers and seen the stipulations and all the requirements and all those wretched get-up-and-go phrases they keep using, I knew I'd really finished with that kind of thing. I just couldn't face it, because it was going to take too long, and anyway, you've got to remember that I'd just left a firm where I'd done a lot of the hiring and firing. I was tired of trying to create an impression.

'I put the money in a bank in my own neighbourhood. It was rather easy, because all I did was walk in and ask the clerk for a form to open an account, and he referred me to the manager. I thought he would do that. One thing I had been anticipating they would ask for and that was a reference. Most of the banks like to be able to refer to other banks for a reference. It's like an old boys' club, but all it does is establish that you are known elsewhere. It's absolutely nothing to do with your character. The banks are not really interested in people at all, only in the deposits, which they use for investment purposes. It's an irony that they all lend money which isn't their own property in the first place and they buy the pound at one price and sell it at about 400 per cent on cost. But that's the way of money lenders the world over, isn't it? Oh yes, I'd done a lot of homework on the banks and their systems . . .

'Well, the manager came out to sell the sort of confidence they specialize in. The whole thing is based on confidence. At college, when I was reading economics, I was always intrigued by the fact that people rarely withdraw all their money from an account. What the banks do is make something out of nothing, because everything is done by cheques. If you're in banking, you know that a cheque means nothing except the transfer of funds, and those funds don't really exist as buildings and the solid sort of assets exist. They are purely and simply ledger entries. Just look at the money position in any town or city. Wages are paid on Friday. On Saturday most of the wage money is spent with local shopkeepers, and the shopkeepers bring it all back to the bank. Full circle! I know it's all very elementary, but once you get the hang of it, the holy cow image of banking just dissolves. Believe me, the banks are on to a very good thing and they always have been, and it will probably go on until we stumble on to a new system. In the weeks I was lazing about without much to do, I couldn't help thinking about all this. You see, we take the banks so much for granted, but they are based on nothing at all. Has it ever struck you, for instance, that the big banks—the Big Five—don't pay any interest at all on current accounts? You can imagine what the total of current accounts must amount to. Yet the banks make the fullest use of the money in the current accounts, even if they do have to obey the rules and retain about 90 per cent against demand. And who lays down the rules but the Bank of England? They are self-governing, they don't stand for any government intervention, we don't know what they are up to half the time. What it boils down to is that the banks can use a percentage of current deposits for various purposes, and at any given moment that must run into thousands of millions of pounds. Now, what I wanted was some of that money, and, as I saw it, I wasn't really going to take it in hard cash . . .

'As a matter of fact, when you open a new bank account, they don't always insist on a reference as a matter of course, and that applies especially when you walk in with a large cash deposit. When I put mine down on the manager's desk, I could see him wondering why I hadn't simply instructed my previous bank to close the account and transfer the balance, but I'd already thought of that one, and I said I'd been considering making a cash deposit on a business and a house, but it had all fallen through at the last moment, hence the cash, which I had been holding in readiness for the deal. He accepted this and I said he could, of course, apply to my previous bank for a reference, although I didn't name it and he didn't ask me, so there it was, and he didn't know a thing about me.

'All well and good. That was stage one completed. The profits due from my partnership were paid to me, and it was more than enough to see me through the next six months. At first I didn't really think I would be able to occupy myself. I was at a loss, so I made up my mind to cultivate some new interests. It was quite unlike me, but I got interested in keeping fish and I set up some tanks in my basement. It's a fascinating subject, you know. I spent hours, fiddling about, and I even started travelling quite long distances for a certain kind of fish I wanted. Time flew by. This six-month wait was purely to let my new bank account settle down. I kept calling in once or twice a week, withdrawing small sums and putting a bit in, and I was always asking the manager's advice about some mythical deal I was thinking of doing. What I was doing was becoming part of the furniture, so to speak.

'Then in the seventh month I rented a cheap bedsitter in another area, about fifteen miles away. I established myself there under another name, and I even went to the length of wearing some old clothes, and I told my landlady that I expected to be away working for several days at a time. It's really quite incredible how people will accept you if a story sounds real enough. If I'd told her I was a professional snake charmer, I'm quite sure she would have accepted it. Anyway, what I did tell her was that I was a landscape gardener. That happened to be a subject I knew something about—in theory, at least. She even got me to have a look at her garden and give her some free advice. When I asked her if she knew of a local bank I could use, she was very ready to help me. Luckily, it wasn't a branch of my own bank, so I went and saw the manager, and I said that my landlady had recommended me, so it seemed to please him no end. As I'd supposed, he did want a reference before he could take my account, so I gave him my real name and address, and, as you might expect, a letter duly arrived at my house a few days later, asking for the reference. I got quite a lot of enjoyment out of saying that Mr So-and-So, the landscape gardener, was a man with the highest qualifications and was of impressive integrity, and to my personal knowledge commanded extremely healthy fees for his work, being a consistent worker, blah-blah. I signed it and posted it, and so by the time I got back to the area, there was a letter of acceptance from the bank waiting for me. It was all so easy. . . . You know, anybody who wants to establish accounts with fifty banks on this sort of basis could do it. There's absolutely nothing to it, and it's not illegal, either. I'd already drawn some money out of the first account in cash, so I paid it in at once to the new one. It was only £50, just to start it off. I paid £50 in cash every ten days, regular as clockwork, until I was up to about £1,000. The only thing that worried me was the interest. Then my new manager suggested I might like to put some of the money into a special account where it would earn a certain guaranteed rate of interest if it stayed where it was for a five-year term. At that time the rate of interest would have been more than £15 a year, and it would have been automatically notified to the Inland Revenue by the bank, so I somehow wriggled out of that by telling him I often needed ready cash in my line of business, so he gave up.

'I don't mind telling you, I got quite a shock when he broadly hinted that he'd always wanted his own garden landscaping by an expert like me. He got so insistent about it that I just had to go round to his house one Sunday for lunch and have a look at his garden. Beautiful place he had, very well kept, but too much lawn. It really wasn't very difficult to suggest that it would be quite a big job. What I was trying to do was put him off. I didn't like the man, because he was so obviously after something for nothing, although I had to keep on his side for the time being. It was very fortunate that he and his wife happened to be going on a cruise for a fortnight, because in the end I said I'd landscape his garden for him. As soon as he was away, I hired a landscaping firm from another district. I didn't say it wasn't my garden, they simply assumed it was. They finished the job in ten days, and I sat on a garden seat and watched them doing it. Then I paid their bill in cash and that was that. The place was a picture. When he came back he thought so, too, and I wouldn't take a penny for it. You could see him glowing at the thought of getting something for nothing. Well, if it did nothing else, it did get him on my side, and that's all I really needed.

'A few weeks later I called in to ask him for a small overdraft. It was only £150 and he granted it without question. I paid it all off in about two-thirds of the agreed time, using my other account to do it, and some time later I asked him for another one. Same thing all over again. Then I planned the big one. During this period I took some large sums out of the first account and put them in the second one until I had about £4,000.

'When I was in brokerage I did learn one rather important fact, and it was that any document is generally taken at its face value provided there is no glaring reason to question it. If you show a man a one-million pound note, he might be curious and even incredulous, but he will accept the fact that it is a one-million pound note. Just look at forged references, look at the way ledgers are cooked for the auditors—there must be dozens of examples. I soon reached the conclusion that I would have to produce something for the bank manager to see, but it was even more important to prepare the man himself. I started mentioning that I was trying to secure a contract for landscaping several dozen hotels throughout the country, and all of them were run by the same company. I pointed out that while I undoubtedly knew my job, I had to admit that I was still only a very small business man and I certainly didn't have enough resources to hire enough men and machines for the contract. Of course, just as I expected, the bank manager jollied me along. He said he thought I ought to be bold! Why didn't I go ahead and tender for the job? The bank might be able to help me with a short-term loan. Another few weeks went by and I was still paying in about £50 at a time. Of course, my original account was quite dented by this time, but the thing was being done to a timetable, it was all part of the plan.

'I mentioned the respect which people seem to have for documents. In order to do it properly, I needed a document, and to get it I had to visit one of the hotels in the group I mentioned to the bank manager, and I found some letterheads in the writing room. I slightly changed the name of the parent company, which was used in very small lettering, and I used some white retouching paint to blot out the regional address, then I found a back-street printer to produce a few hundred copies for me. It was done by offset-litho. It's a very useful method, because it gives you an exact copy of the original. He didn't even question it. He just took the cash and gave me a receipt. I went home—my real home—and got in touch with a firm that was selling a new kind of electric typewriter, and they sent their salesman along to see me. After four stiff scotches and a lot of talk, he agreed to lend me a model overnight so that I could try it out for myself. I sat up late that night, carefully drafting a very convincing contract for the landscaping job and mentioning a fat fee for the job in the region of £12,500. I folded it and posted it to myself under my other name at the other address, and as soon as it came back I took it along to the bank. He didn't even look at it properly except to make a note of the figures.

'Have you ever come across that saying they use in fund-raising circles: think big, ask big? It's absolutely right. Ask for a million and you'll get it, but ask for a hundred and they'll probably show you the door. He drew up the papers on the spot, I signed them and that was that, and as I walked out of his office, I realized that banking is based absolutely and completely on trust, simply on the face value of the customer. Good old-fashioned values. I think we are going to see more of it, too, especially as this American method of credit rating gets a foothold over here. It's bound to change things considerably. I thought about all this a great deal while I was in prison, and it seemed to me that a really clever operator could move much faster than any centralized computer control, although I admit it's probably the sort of thing you could do only once, so it would have to be big enough to make it worthwhile . . .

'Supposing a syndicate of twenty people agreed to work for a set fee for an organizer who wanted to raise about £20,000 in a single day. It is by no means impossible to do it once you have established individual credit ratings. Multiply it by fifty or a hundred. It's a distinct possibility. The only danger in waiting is when you are waiting for nothing at all. But in an operation of the kind I am talking about, the waiting time is the planning time, and when you have hour after hour on your hands in prison, you start thinking about what you might do when you get out of the place. I don't think it will be long before the old style of bank robbery with coshes, masks and ammonia becomes as out of date as steam engines, especially when it dawns on somebody that a huge cash-credit operation is limited only by the number of people in it. Even one person could do surprisingly well for ready cash if he first of all established a modest credit rating and a card to make cash withdrawals of up to, say, £30 at any branch through the country. Imagine calling at three branches during one morning in neighbouring towns and drawing £30 at each of them. That makes £90. You would probably be able to go on for at least five days and that would make £450. Of course, £450 isn't very much nowadays, but just let your imagination run on. Supposing you make credit arrangements with five different banks and you made withdrawals at all of them and their branches during a period of five days. You would make £2,250. You can be absolutely sure that by the middle of the second week your name would be circularized in all directions. Obviously, the whole art of this is being able to do it very quickly. You could probably do even better than this because the cash availability industry is growing all the time, and you can cash cheques much more easily nowadays, because most of the banks provide cheque indemnity to the limit of about £30. Look at these cash dispensers outside banks these days. It won't be long before they are in front of every bank in the country. You can get £10 at a time out of them. I seriously believe that if a clever person used all these methods at once, he should be able to make at least £10,000 within five days, all in hard cash. But it does call for intensive organization. That's why a good business background can be so helpful in these matters.

'However, there I was with a credit of nearly £12,500. You could go mad with that kind of money, and I must say I was tempted to have a binge and go out on the town, buy myself a car, find a pretty girl, but it would have been so damned conventional, and it didn't quite appeal to me. After all, it's the sort of thing pools winners do, isn't it? That night I went to the cinema, but quite honestly I didn't pay much attention to the film and I sat through it twice before I went out and had a meal at a cheap café. Strange how these things take you, but I suddenly had a hankering for bacon and eggs, and that's exactly what I did have. Twice.

'During the next few weeks I went through a rather harrowing phase. Basically, what I wanted to do was maintain the confidence of the second bank while depleting the £12,500. One doesn't simply wade in and withdraw the whole sum in three or four moves. That would cause some concern. The best way of doing it by allowing the account to ebb and flow, so to speak. I even mustered about £100 from my original account and paid it into bank number two in two separate payments before I started things moving. Then I finally started using the overdraft, a little at a time over a few weeks, then in larger amounts, until I had about £3,000 in all. I then paid in £2,500 to bank number two. The one thing which you have to remember is that overdrafts of this size are scrutinized very carefully every week by the manager and, in turn, he is answerable to the bank inspector, who normally turns up at regular intervals to check the books. Experienced bank managers are told to use their discretion up to a certain figure, but beyond that figure they have to obtain sanction from head office, and these are the very accounts which the travelling bank inspectors watch very closely. That was why I juggled about with the money, taking some out and putting some back, but not quite all of it was put in. The inevitable result over a period of about one year was that I transferred practically all of the £12,000 into my account with bank number one. For the last two or three months of this operation I didn't go near the overdraft bank. There was no need to, because I knew that it was only a matter of time before head office started putting some pressure on the manager to chase me up for regular payments. At that point I left my lodgings and went back home and there I waited. I did take one small precaution and that was to hold enough ready cash in case of emergencies, and as soon as I had settled in again, I was able to resume a fairly leisurely life, so there was no need to go anywhere near a bank.

'The crisis took a lot longer to come to a head than you might think, then one day I had a telephone call and it turned out to be the manager of the bank number two. He said that as I had acted as a referee for the landscape gardener, he would like to see me about it if I could spare him a few minutes. I just grunted through a handkerchief at him, and he said he would call during the afternoon. I wish you could have seen his face when I opened the door and invited him in. Have you ever heard the American saying about somebody being completely thrown? He just stood there with his mouth hanging open, trying to force the obvious question, and before he could utter a word, I had him in the lounge with a glass of sherry in his hand. Of course, he realized like a flash what had gone wrong. The first thing he said was: "You simply must pay it back, every damned penny of it" and he kept saying the same thing over and over again until I had to interrupt him and tell him point blank that it was quite out of the question. He just wouldn't have it and he could do whatever he liked about it. And then he started getting angry, very angry indeed, and he said it would cause no end of top-level trouble with head office, and I was bound to be interviewed by senior officials. This discussion had been going on in my mind for months. I knew what he was going to say and I knew what he was going to do, and then he started getting rather pressing about what I'd done with his money. He kept calling it his money, and I must say I found it very amusing. When I said I hadn't done anything with it, I did make a small mistake, because I needn't have said anything. He was with me for three or four hours, arguing and cajoling, and when I finally got rid of him, I saw him rush across the road to the telephone box, and he was in there for about twenty minutes, making one call after another. Poor fellow, he was in a terrible state. I went out that evening and I enjoyed myself.

'Although the banks like people to infer that they are in some kind of competition, and they go to great lengths to attract custom, they seem to subscribe to some kind of common intelligence network, because it was only three or four days before they discovered the existence of my other bank acount, and then I had a visit from a little fellow who said he was the deputy head of security of bank number two. I rather liked him, because he was very civil and dispassionate about it, and he didn't get at all excited. A most reasonable man. First of all, he established that my two identities related to one person. I agreed that this was so, and I had also given myself a very good reference. Then he said they had discovered that I had £12,000 in a certain bank. Was this the sum of the overdraft? I said I would prefer not to go into the matter. He didn't press me about it, and off he went. The next day the manager of the first bank turned up and went over the whole business again. He said it was all very embarrassing, because I was a client of the bank. I didn't admit that the £12,000 which he was looking after was the overdraft money. After all, one pound note looks very much like any other pound note, doesn't it?'

At this point a very interesting situation developed. In a series of secret meetings between the representatives of the two banks, great endeavours were made to decide what should be done. It was initially assumed by bank number two that bank number one would cheerfully hand back the £12,000, thereby enabling them to close the matter and save face, and it is quite possible that Mr X would never have seen the inside of a prison. As it happened, however, bank number one invoked the cardinal rule of secrecy between bank and customer. Although the amounts of money involved happened to be identical, this did not necessarily imply that it was the same money. No doubt something could have been established by means of serial numbers and dates, but monies paid in are not checked by serial number, only by amount.

Each bank realized that a condition of stalemate had been reached. The only solution was to seek legal advice. What emerged from this was that while bank number one could theoretically be charged with aiding and abetting if bank number two could prove the case, such a charge would be ludicrous. Although the security officers of both banks desperately tried to confine the investigation so that all discussions were held in conditions of total secrecy, the unusual nature of the whole business and the obvious need for a rapid solution caused the directors of the banks to hold their own meetings. At one time several different meetings were being held on the same day by the various interests. In this period Mr X continued his leisurely life, looking after his fish and realizing that some kind of nemesis must inevitably overtake him. It was, as they say, only a matter of time, although time itself conspired to aid him, and it was several more weeks before the banks were able to agree on a collective statement of events for the benefit of an eminent barrister. The author of several standard legal works and no longer practising due to an affluence created by his appearance in several major cases, he agreed to give an opinion on the understanding that he would not be expected to conduct any case which might come to court. His astronomical fee was paid in advance and the papers were despatched by special messenger to his home. Three weeks later there was no sign of the promised opinion. By this time both banks were naturally taut with expectation. A tentative enquiry was sent to the great man. It remained unanswered. A telephone call to his home by a senior bank official brought forth the information that he was on holiday in Vienna. His secretary said that he had taken the case papers with him. She helpfully supplied the telephone number and the address of the hotel in Vienna. Yet another telephone call was made. The barrister was easily located. Yes, he said, he had formed an opinion and he would be writing shortly. The bank official explained that time was now running short. Could he perhaps give some hint on the phone? There was a long pause and the barrister then said: 'Yes—yes, I think so, if you'd like to hear it. In the first place the laddie who engineered this affair was damned clever. No attempt at running away, no real proof as far as the origin of the money was concerned. There's nothing illegal about changing your name, provided it's done for legal reasons. He was a landscape gardener under his other name, he banked money under that name. He changed the hotel company letterhead, you say, so you could say that while he forged an instrument for fraudulent purposes, he did not do anything of the kind, because the company on the letterhead he used did not exist. You cannot impersonate something that doesn't exist. Of course, misrepresentation might hold water in court, but I wouldn't be too happy about it. I could have some precedents looked up—'

'Is that all?' asked the bank official, hardly believing what he had heard.

'Well, what else is there to it?' demanded the barrister.

'Great God in heaven, this man has stolen £12,000!'

'As the case appears to me, I would rather doubt the legal accuracy of that statement.'

'What? But surely the circumstantial—'

'No, old chap, it would not hold water. The only salient point is the origin of the money. It was loaned in good faith. I must say I'm rather surprised at the lack of collateral. Wish my bank was as helpful. . . . However, the bank that loaned him the money could bankrupt him—'

But banks are loath to bankrupt their clients, whatever the circumstances. It tarnishes their avuncular image.

The barrister continued: 'The only thing I can recommend with any degree of certainty is that you prosecute the chap for plain straightforward fraud. But it is definitely a risk. It means coming out with the whole ghastly story in open court. Makes the banks look foolish. But if you want to risk it—'

After further agonizing meetings it was finally decided to follow his advice. The papers were prepared. In the meantime, an unofficial meeting was held with the police to determine whether the case might be passed to them for criminal proceedings to be instigated, but after examining eight files full of papers, they declined on the basis that this seemed to be a case of civil debt.

Mr X appeared in court. The case occupied three long hot

June days, in which time Mr X was cross examined for less than twenty minutes, although both bank managers spent several hours in the witness box, followed by senior security officials, who went to great pains to elucidate the method used by Mr X to acquire the money. At one point the manager of bank number two suffered some embarrassing moments when he was forced to admit that Mr X had landscaped his garden free of charge. The judge took a penetrating interest in this and wanted to know whether there was any question of favour being returned for favour. Throughout the trial the judge made copious notes and asked many questions. He alone was apparently impervious to the oppressive heat of the courtroom. It took only two days for him to prepare a summation in which he stated that while he had serious doubts about many of the accusations made by the prosecution, he was nevertheless satisfied that a fraud of sorts had been perpetrated by Mr X. Despite this, he was perfectly satisfied that bank number one was within its rights in refusing to relinquish the sum of £12,000, which now reposed in the deposit account of the accused. It was, he added, a domestic matter for the banks to settle between themselves, but to his mind the traditional secrecy between bank and client must be maintained at all costs. There was no evidence to suggest the origin of the money which Mr X had deposited in either of his accounts, and evidence on this point had not been adequately presented.

Mr X was sentenced to two years' imprisonment, and he was freed in something less than that time. His first move was to transfer his bank account to a branch in central London, and it was later moved to a Paris bank. Only a year or two later he engineered the same fraud all over again, this time using banks in Paris and Marseille, and trebling his capital in the process. The case received very little newspaper attention, but the judge professed himself to be slightly amused as he sent Mr X to prison for one year.

Index